MW01007949

THE
FIVE LOST
SUPERPOWERS

THE

FIVE LOST
SUPERPOWERS

WHY WE LOSE THEM AND
HOW TO GET THEM BACK

. . . . .

JOHN REID   ANDREW REID

CORENA CHASE   LYNAE STEINHAGEN

LIONCREST
PUBLISHING

The Five Lost Superpowers
Why We Lose Them and How to Get Them Back

ISBN 978-1-5445-2294-4 *Hardcover*
       978-1-5445-2292-0 *Paperback*
       978-1-5445-2293-7 *Ebook*

CONTENTS

* * * * *

*This book is dedicated
to the superheroes all around us—
those who fight for justice, seek the truth,
and take personal risks for
the greater good.*

* * * * *

FOREWORD

Ben hunches there, teetering on the top bar of the jungle gym. Although he and his brothers, Jacob and Christian, came to the playground alone, they're now fully immersed in a universe of Dragons and Dinosaurs.

Ben, a Dragon, appears cornered. A few Dinosaurs are poised around and down the slide. To the right, near the monkey bars, another cluster of Dinosaurs are encouraging Ben to come their way so that they can capture him, as they have the other Dragons, who are languishing on the swings. Ben yells to his compatriots, "Don't worry, I will rescue you!"

It looks like if Ben can find a way to free the other Dragons, the game can continue. His grandfather, or any other observer over sixty years old with bad knees, couldn't anticipate Ben's next move: he decides to jump down from the top of the jungle gym and make a run for the swings. Perhaps he's misjudged how hard the ground can be; he tumbles and, for a moment, sprawls on the dusty field. The looming Dinosaurs, shocked by the move, step back and freeze. Ben quickly brushes himself off and races to free the Dragons. The Dinosaurs, in hot pursuit, ultimately get the remaining Dragon.

After a short breather, there's a quick huddle about the next round and whether they should "keep the same teams."

Later, Jacob and Christian join Ben and their grandfather, Pa, as they amble out of the playground. Pa tests his understanding of the game against his observations.

"So. It's called Dragons and Dinosaurs."

"Yep," Ben replies. "I was a Dragon, and Jacob and Christian were Dinosaurs."

"Actually," Jacob interrupts, "I was a T-Rex, and Christian was a Microraptor. Dinosaurs are the best."

"You know dinosaurs and dragons didn't ever really fight, right?" Pa asks.

"Of course they didn't. Dragons aren't real," Jacob continues.

"I think if they did coexist, the dragons would clearly have won," Pa insists.

"No, Pa, dinosaurs are way bigger and tougher," Jacob and Christian say, almost in unison.

Ben quickly counters that "dragons are far more clever and faster!"

"Dragons have magical powers! I think dragons would win," Pa says, voicing his opinion.

"Pa," Jacob says with a touch of disappointment, "no dragon could beat a T-Rex in a fight."

Ben, sensing Pa is in way over his head, shifts gears. "What game did you play as a kid?"

"We played a game called Sardines."

"How did it go?" asks Ben.

"One person is 'it' and runs and hides. The other players count to sixty and then go looking for the person who is 'it.' They do it by themselves. The first person who finds them…"

"... wins," Ben and Jacob say together.

"No. He or she just quietly sits or lies next to them until everyone else eventually finds them."

"Wow, that sounds boring. You would just lay there until the last person finds you? Why is it called Sardines?" asks Jacob.

"Sardines are a type of fish that come in a can, packed really close together."

"Canned fish? Yuck! Dragons and dinosaurs are much better," Christian says, while Ben and Jacob nod in agreement.

I am that grandfather. Piqued by my grandsons' questions, I did some research. Dragons do have superpowers: in Western culture, they're able to breathe fire; in Eastern culture, they can control water, rainfall, hurricanes, and floods.[1]

Children have superpowers of their own. These are key to helping them grow and adapt. Ben, Jacob, and Christian exhibited five of the many superpowers observed in children:

Playfulness (Dragons and Dinosaurs.)

Compassion ("Don't worry, I will rescue you!")

Resilience (He brushes himself off and runs to free the others.)

Curiosity ("Why is it called Sardines?")

Authenticity ("Wow, that sounds boring.")

These superpowers burn bright in children. When we see children exercise these powers, we end up smiling and laughing and, invariably, telling other adults about it. We react like we have just seen lightning captured in a bottle, something rare, since we do not get to witness these powers in our day-to-day adult world.

As of this writing, the Marvel Cinematic Universe is the highest-grossing film franchise in history.[2] Part of the attraction of its multiple superheroes is the dream possibility that we—children of all ages—could be one of them. That we, too, could save the day, defeat villains, and stand tall for truth and justice. That we would survive and ultimately prevail over villains' slings and arrows. And while superheroes may possess superhuman abilities, most also possess important qualities available to virtually everyone.

The good news is while many adults may not exercise these powers, most of us haven't abandoned them entirely. Much like Dorothy in Oz, whom Glinda told, "You've always had the power,"[3] we can still draw on these talents from within ourselves. The strategy to finding them, like locating a set of lost keys, begins with retracing our steps. By understanding when we last had them and where we lost them, we can reignite them.

We have gathered our own version of the Fantastic Four to reignite these superpowers. You will find that each author has their own voice, but we all have a passion for helping people be the best versions of themselves.

Our goal—our hope—for ourselves and you is to make the case that these superpowers matter because they make us human (not super). The essence of our humanity is at the center of everything good in the working world and beyond. When we're in touch with it, we can make great leaps in a single bound.

So, find your own Fortress of Solitude, and let's explore each of these five superpowers. We'll examine how children demonstrate and express them, what happens to them as children move toward adulthood, their value, and, finally, what we can do to unleash them within ourselves.

CHAPTER ONE

. . . . .

CURIOSITY

WELCOME TO EARTH

In what can only be described as a miracle (given the odds), you were born! Do you realize what has to happen for you to be born and the chances you came out as you? The odds of you being born as you may be as much as **1 in 400 trillion**.[4] Welcome to Earth!

You were born with no cape, no lasso of truth, not even a heart-shaped herb from Wakanda. While you were pretty much naked, you did have one thing going for you: you were born wildly curious. From the moment you showed up, there you were, studying shapes, sounds, movements, colors, and textures. You explored both verbal and nonverbal language. You approached the world constantly testing a hypothesis that your little brain had concocted—"I can eat this block. I can ride this dog. I can touch this paint." You were the head of Research and Development for You, Inc.

Theorists and empiricists have worked hard to understand childhood curiosity and have come up with a variety of ways to define it. Studies in the field use terms like *incongruity theory*, *ambiguity aversion*, *effectance motivation*, and *ocular lust*, to name a few.

Susan Engel, author of *The Hungry Mind* and a leading international authority on curiosity in children, says it best, "I would suggest that curiosity is simply the urge to know more."[5]

As an infant, your curiosity superpower is, well, in its infancy. You have not reached your full superpower as an infant because your language skills are of little help in your pursuit of knowledge. You're simply Tony Stark or Bruce Wayne before they suit up.

It is when we become toddlers and are able to ask questions that our curiosity superpower reaches its zenith. It is questions, and how we structure and deliver them, that demonstrate true curiosity.

In 2007, researchers logging questions asked by children aged fourteen months to five years found they asked an average of 107 questions an hour. One child asked three questions a minute at his peak. That's Hulk-level curiosity.[6]

In their free exploration, children can pose delightful questions:

- If I have two eyes, how come I can only see one thing at a time?

- How did the first people make tools when there were no tools?

- Why don't spiders get stuck in their own webs?

- What if bees could talk?

Children are not inhibited by adult mental and emotional baggage (feeling shame, fearing embarrassment, feigning confidence). Children are not told nonsense like, "Fake it 'til you make it" or "Hold your questions until the end." If they are raised in a healthy environment, their curiosity and questions are rewarded. However, almost imperceptibly, their curiosity superpower is under attack.

Thomas Szasz, a Hungarian-American academic, psychiatrist, and psychoanalyst, makes it clear: "Every act of conscious learning requires the willingness to suffer an injury to one's self-esteem. That is why young children, before they are aware of their own self-importance, learn so easily."[7]

CURIOSITY'S KRYPTONITE

The attack on curiosity is not a direct blow. It's a combination of the stories we tell, the emphasis society places on knowing, and the impact of technology—and, of course, we can always blame our parents.

Many of us are familiar with the story from Genesis of Adam and Eve and their fall from grace. God created paradise but with one critical catch: "Of every tree of the garden you may freely eat; but of the tree of the knowledge of good and evil you shall not eat, for in the day that you eat of it you shall surely die." (Gen. 2:16–17 New King James Version). As we know, the serpent argues with Eve that God is withholding something of value. Both Eve and Adam end up partaking of the fruit.

One obvious villain in this piece is the serpent. Biblical scholars tell us the story is about obedience to the Lord and the consequences of defiance. Other scholars make humanity's "greed" the culprit: we were in paradise yet went after the one thing we could not have. I would argue the unseen villain is curiosity: "When the woman saw that the fruit of the tree was good for food and pleasing to the eye, *and also desirable for gaining wisdom*, she took some and ate it." (Gen. 3:6 New International Version).

There are many lessons from the Adam and Eve story, but it is hard to see how one of them cannot be that curiosity and wisdom are devilish pursuits. Saint Augustine himself said that "God fashioned hell for the inquisitive."

A familiar saying goes that "curiosity killed the cat." And sadly, the injunction against curiosity builds from there, particularly for pre-K girls. Time and again, like Sleeping Beauty or Goldilocks, a young girl's curiosity places her in peril. Then at age five, kids are swept off to school to get an education, where they learn that being well-behaved is more prized than being Dora the Explorer. The clear lesson is "mind your own business; keep your head down."

Educators' preference for well-behaved students is understandable: they consider it necessary to the environment for learning. Couple this with lesson plans directed toward a clearly defined, often-narrow end point, and you have a country of classrooms that discourage off-topic curiosity.

In *The Hungry Mind,* Engel and her research team discovered that questioning drops like a stone once children start school. They found that the youngest children in an American suburban elementary school asked only between two and five questions in a two-hour period. Worse, as they grew older, the children gave up asking questions altogether. There were two-hour stretches in fifth grade (year six) in which ten- and eleven-year-olds asked their teacher not a single question.[8]

Learning, therefore, is not defined as an adventure; it's not even a search. It's a finite game: learn this, now go learn that, and don't ask anything along the way, just take in what you're told. Learning devolves to a means serving an end. The end is grades; the means are the "right" answers.

Society rewards this emphasis on knowing. We are told that knowledge is power. Expressions such as, "Don't ask a question if you don't know the answer" pass for wisdom.

Meanwhile, back inside the home, two sources of kryptonite are hidden in plain sight. Parents tend not to question in service of curiosity but rather to get the behavior they want. All over the world, parents offer questions like:

- Are you sure you want to hang out with those kids?

- Don't you think you should be doing your homework?

- Have you considered wearing a jacket?

Statements hidden in questions teach that questions are about getting the answers we want. Questions aren't used in service of curiosity but rather for thinly veiled advocacy and manipulation. (We also get to pick up a little about passive-aggressive behavior, but that's for another book.)

Also, paradoxically, technology curses curiosity. On its face, it would appear technology is a boon to inquiry. It offers access to so much available information with relatively little effort. To paraphrase a famous children's book, "Oh, the keys we can click and the things we will learn!" Not so fast.

First, we have outsourced our curiosity to search engines. Search engines are extremely forgiving of poorly asked questions. A couple of words loosely thrown together can deliver us the answer we seek. What's the problem? This gradually weakens our ability to ask good questions, which are curiosity's muscles.

Thanks to technology, we also begin to think we are smarter than we are because once we find information, we tell ourselves, "I knew that." Believing we know stuff that we, in fact, do not know depresses curiosity.

Finally, technology thrives on identifying and then marketing, or, more accurately, pandering, to our *existing beliefs*. One tragedy of the adult human condition is that we would rather form an opinion and then reinforce it than consider other views and—"Holy cow, Batman!"—perhaps change our own perspective.

INCURIOUS IN A VUCA WORLD

We are now adults in the working world—a highly volatile, uncertain, complex, challenging, and ambiguous one in which the future belongs to the learners. Just when we need our five-year-old childlike curiosity the most, its heart is barely beating.

If we get a job that requires us to influence others (sales, consulting, or any influence role), we might become only quasi-curious because our curiosity about the other person is limited to achieving our goals. Everything is tied to driving an outcome, so we reduce our questions to a series of transactions instead of building true understanding. Remember, our education makes curiosity a means to an end.

We are told to be really good at something. A common saying warns against being "a jack of all trades, master of none." The implication is that a range of knowledge is of little value. Specialized expertise, we are told, should be our goal. But is this true for the majority of us?

In *Outliers,* Malcolm Gladwell suggests the 10,000-hour rule: practice something for 10,000 hours, become an expert, and success will follow. He wrongly hypothesized that expertise is the key to success.[9] In his book *Range,* David Epstein states there is growing evidence that if you operate in a "kind" learning and functioning environment, where the rules are clear and the patterns are fairly easy to grasp, deep expertise, the 10,000-hour rule, and grit will serve you well.[10] This is an environment where if you learn how to do this, then that, and then this, it will definitely lead to success. Becoming a world-class specialist is the key to success in such an environment.

However, more and more, we live in a disruptive, or what is called a "wicked," learning and functioning environment. In this environment, the keys are to learn more broadly and widely, pursue different career paths, and build expertise and knowledge outside your "field."

So, here we are exposed. We know something—and we know it deeply. This depth of knowledge in one area will only take us so far, though. We are Batman with one tool in our toolbelt—and it is Bat Shark Repellant, which, we can all agree, has limited value.

The complete saying is actually, "A **jack of all trades** is a master of none, **but oftentimes better than a master of one**." It turns out the balance of the quote is far more prescient in the environment in which we find ourselves.

In the wicked learning environment, where the issues are more complex, the targets are moving, and you're not sure what to learn next to succeed at this moment, you've got some experimenting, learning, and trial-and-erroring to do. Becoming a world-class generalist in such an environment is increasingly shown to be the better path to success.

If science is your calling, strive for broadness throughout your career. Students who take an interdisciplinary array of science courses are better at thinking analytically. Researchers with off-beat knowledge combinations score more "hit" papers. Nobel laureates in science are more likely than their less-recognized peers—twenty-two times more likely!—to have artistic pursuits outside their field.[11]

SUPERPOWER IN ACTION

I witnessed a leader in a global consulting practice tell a group of newly minted college graduates that their focus and goal should be to identify and hone "their fastball." The argument was all about becoming an indispensable specialist and expert. The cynic in me thought, "Of course that's his advice. He is focused solely on billable hours and believes that the firm can more quickly monetize these shiny new employees if they are experts."

My own experience counters this idea of everyone pursuing a specialty, and I am more convinced that you need to have a broad range of skills—a curveball and a changeup, if you will. Within the consulting firm, there are many examples of people with depth and breadth who now lead the global practice. Ironically, the leader who was speaking has a bio that is wide and varied.

At university, I majored in economics. At that time, Dow Chemical was more interested in hiring graduates with strong interpersonal skills than technical skills. While I had never taken a chemistry course in my life and could barely tell you the difference between inorganic and organic chemicals, Dow made me an offer, and I accepted.

Most of my peers had deep technical backgrounds, many with chemical engineering degrees. My approach to selling chemicals was significantly different than theirs. I was genuinely curious about all parts of my clients' operations: the tanks they used, the temperatures they ran at, how they handled waste—all of which was new to me and genuinely interesting.

My peers, with their fancy chemical backgrounds, were more interested in showing the client what they knew, meanwhile avoiding subjects they didn't know. The ideas of being a learner, being curious, and being vulnerable were not how they thought they would succeed.

So, while my colleagues were expounding, I was asking questions and listening, and I found out what we all know: people love to talk about themselves. Technically trained plant managers really appreciated the opportunity to share about their process. My interest was real, and so their interest, when it was my turn to speak, was magnified. Knowledge, it turns out, may be power if that knowledge involves demonstrating curiosity.

TOOLBELT: REGAINING YOUR CURIOSITY SUPERPOWER

What does curiosity look like in adults? If it is the desire to know, then the desire to know what? Fortunately, the latest research gives us a robust understanding, identifying five types of curiosity that can be assessed:[12]

- Sensory deprivation (discomfort with not knowing something)

- Joyous exploration (love of learning)

- Overt social curiosity (open interest in others)

- Covert social curiosity (indirect, surreptitious, and secretive interest)

- Thrill-seeking (physical risk-taking)

It is the first three of these that, as leaders, we can and should reignite. Let's jump into that phone booth and put the Curiosity **C.A.P.E.** back on.

CAST A WIDE NET.

Bertrand Russell argued that the best way to overcome the fear of death is to make your interests gradually wider and more impersonal until, bit by bit, the walls of the ego recede.[13] A loss of curiosity is its own kind of death.

We can embrace Russell's thinking and bravely seek wider and more disparate sources of information. We can broaden what we read, listen to, and watch. Visiting only those websites with which we agree can be, apologies to Snickers, just a sugar high. What will really satisfy curiosity is to expand our boundaries and, like a curious Aquaman or Aquawoman, cast a wider net for a disparate set of fish.

Exposing ourselves to diverse sources of fiction can have a powerful effect as well. There is some truth and some superhero magic to the saying, "A reader lives a thousand lives before they die." Fictional stories allow us to explore and discover the world before, during, and, potentially, after us. A story's narrative flow and the types of stories told are all designed to capture and maintain our curiosity. A growing body of research finds that people who read fiction tend to better understand and share in the feelings of others—even those who are different from themselves.[14]

ASK BETTER QUESTIONS.

Clearly, we have to let go of what our parents have taught us. This cockamamie idea of suppressing questions we don't know the answer to needs to stop. We channel our parents when we ask questions that start with "Wouldn't you agree...?" or "Don't you think...?"

Over 71 percent of top CEOs admit to being unsure and uncertain about the best path forward—basically, they have their doubts. Yet, they deny searching for "expert" consultants that have an "answer" to their challenge.[15]

So, what is it they want? A thinking partner. They want someone to come alongside them and explore this crazy, wicked learning world. If it wasn't for the lack of any insight, and bad table manners, a toddler, with all of their questions, might be perfect. This exploration requires better questions. And what's a better question? It is one that requires the other person to think, evaluate, and speculate. A couple of techniques are worth mentioning:

- **The Extra Question:** This is simply asking an extra question to both signal interest and gain a more meaningful understanding. Phrases such as "Tell me more.," "How so?," "Why do you feel that way?," and others should all be added to your question quiver.

- **Silence and Pause:** Just stop talking. Ask your question, and then be quiet. Give the other person time—and then more time—to elaborate. Remember, *you* asked the question; it's now their turn to speak.

- **Introduce a Third Party:** Frame your question by seeking the perspective of a third party. Replace "What do you think about X?" with "What do you think Y thinks about X?" The other person thinks more deeply by considering another's point of view.

PERSPECTIVE SEEK.

Theory of Mind says that, at a certain age, we begin to understand that another person's knowledge, beliefs, and emotions are different from our own.[16] Overt social curiosity is simply tapping back into this ability from our youth. It's not about being energized around people (extroversion), but rather it's about having a genuine interest in what makes people tick.

So, exactly how does one perspective seek?

First, you acquire a perspective of your own. Congratulations. Look at you with your flashy and interesting perspective. Calm down. What should excite and intrigue you is how others see things differently than you. Get interested. Keep reminding yourself that you are just one person living in a world filled with various points of view.

Second, be in the moment. No one can write a chapter these days, or really understand another person's perspective, without mentioning *mindfulness*. That said—because it's true—mindfulness brings us into the moment so we can deeply listen to others.

Finally, embrace being wrong. Harvey Dent, of Two-Face fame, did both good and evil. You are invariably right about some things and wrong about others. Your growth will come from what you learn, not from what you know.

EXPLORE THEN EXPLOIT.

Cognitive scientists commonly wrestle with what's known as the **explore-exploit** trade-off. When we're **exploring** and gathering information, we're open to new ideas as we experience a childlike enchantment with nuance and details of the present moment.

When we're working to accomplish any task, basic or complex, we're **exploiting** the knowledge we've gained in order to accomplish something. Adult lives are filled with exploiting the knowledge we've gained.

A by-product, we're told, is an explore-and-exploit tension. It can be described as risk-taking, curiosity, optimism, or impulsivity; it's noisy and random. Exploring is all about acquiring knowledge, so children are much better explorers since they are less interested in exploiting the knowledge they're after. To them, exploration is the thrill.

In numerous studies, children are seen to be far more effective at problem-solving when the solution is unclear and much better at identifying unlikely causal relationships. Without the burden of *exploitation*, they're less likely to rush to a solution, suffer from confirmation bias, or get caught up in what researchers call the "learning trap"—the formation of a stable, false belief, even with extensive experience.[17]

Conversely, adults focus on utility, the value of the information, and its use potential. The ability to exploit our knowledge and meanwhile improve both our social standing and our bank account is the thrill. This fervor to exploit makes great sense in a kind learning environment (predictable, with clear rules, etc.), where feedback is quick, and inferences are more likely to prove valid. Wicked learning environments, the world in which most of us now live, with their volatility, uncertainty, and ambiguity, demand the capacity to keep exploring.

ADDITIONAL INSIGHT FROM THE LAB

Jean Piaget, a leading behaviorist, viewed curiosity as the result of a cognitive disequilibrium caused by a child's tendency to assimilate new information into existing cognitive structures. With a minimum number of rigid mental models, you were able to quickly accommodate new information—and the ease at which you learned was enabled by an openness to information and little in the way of a structured belief system.[18]

Piaget, therefore, described curiosity as the urge to explain the unexpected—or understand the unknown. His emphasis is that curiosity requires novelty, but novelty may be insufficient.[19] If you spend time with a young boy or girl who knows and loves, say, dinosaurs, you will notice their curiosity for the subject is endless. Curiosity is sparked by more than just novelty; it also includes an interest in subjects with which one may have deep familiarity. Let's see if a neuroscientist can help here.

Neuroscientist and psychobiologist Jaak Panksepp identified seven basic emotional states equivalent across different species of animals. One of these states, the SEEKING disposition—shared by many animals—drives explorative behaviors, sustains goal-directed activity, promotes anticipatory cognitions, and evokes feelings of positive excitement, which controls reward-learning.[20] We are simply built to seek and get the dopamine payoff when we seek and find. Curiosity has much to do with brain chemistry.

When it comes to defining curiosity, perhaps where you sit is where you stand.

Consider this example from biologist Robert Sapolsky, who provides answers from different experts for the classic query, "Why did the chicken cross the road?":[21]

- If you ask evolutionary biologists, they might say, "The chicken crossed the road because they saw a potential mate on the other side."

- If you ask kinesiologists, they might say, "Because,

for each step, the muscles in the leg contracted and pulled the leg bone forward."

- If you ask neuroscientists, they might say, "Because the neurons in the chicken's brain fired and triggered the movement."

We soon come to believe that the right answer trumps a good question anytime. We also become aware that being told we are smart feels pretty good. After decades of research, world-renowned Stanford University psychologist Carol S. Dweck, Ph.D., discovered two overarching mindsets. People with a *fixed mindset*—those who believe that their and others' abilities are fixed—are less likely to flourish than people with a *growth mindset*—those who believe that abilities can be developed. It is safe to say that childhood education has supported a fixed-mindset approach.[22]

As Dweck notes, "The first thing we studied was the praise that adults give to children. And we found—contrary to popular wisdom—*that when you praise intelligence, it backfires.* It puts kids into a fixed mindset, and right away, they don't want a challenging task."[23] At its essence, when embracing knowing, we reject the unknown.

Curious about the next chapter? That is your superpower telling you to read on.

· · · · ·

CHAPTER TWO

RESILIENCE

THE SECOND SUPERPOWER:
RESILIENCE

What I know for sure is that resilience has many faces. I just have to look around at the people in my life to see some.[24]

Colin is a five-year-old who's had multiple surgeries to repair a heart condition but was determined to learn how to ride a bike. After countless crashes and skinned knees, he's now unstoppable. There's Michael, who, after recovering from drug and alcohol addiction at age nineteen, recently retired after a forty-five-year career helping others find hope and healing from substance abuse. Samantha manages her bipolar disorder with medication and therapy while running a successful small business and raising three children as a single mother. Rod was raised in an environment with chronically ill parents who left him to fend for himself. He earned his degree in environmental engineering, landed his dream job overseas, and recently married his partner. For twenty-five years, Jo was married to an emotionally abusive man, all the while rising through corporate ranks, earning recognition and respect for her talent. After escaping the marriage, she continued to achieve professional success and recently married the love of her life.

Then, there's me. I was psychologically and physically traumatized in early childhood and have experienced depressive episodes throughout my adult life. Today, I have meaningful relationships that fill me with joy, a consulting practice I adore, and a passion for adventure travel that takes me all over the world. Colin, Michael, Samantha, Rod, Jo, and me—we are resilient. Some of us even "live out loud,"[25] as author Émile Zola sought to do. We've proven that, no matter what has happened to us, resilience is possible.

WHAT IS RESILIENCE?

Defining resilience is like peering through a prism to see the light from a single object refract in different ways. The central idea of being resilient is to "bounce back" from adversity, which makes me think of the witty and charming Bouncing Boy, one of DC Comics' lesser-known superheroes. But resilience is not only about bouncing back, and it's definitely not as humorous as Bouncing Boy made it look. Being knocked on your bum, literally or figuratively, doesn't typically allow for a swift rebound. The Hollywood hero might hop back in the saddle, but we mortals scan for broken bones or a shattered heart before moving on. Resilience is actually thought to exist on a continuum that manifests differently throughout our lives. Scientists, psychologists, and medical experts describe resilience more broadly—in both children and adults—as the "process of, capacity for, or outcome of successful adaptation despite challenging or threatening circumstances."[26] In other words: adjust, adapt, and get on with it. For me, there's something lacking in that view of resilience because it's missing how resilience feels. Successful adaptation isn't just about getting through. It's also about making meaning and having a sense of resolve about where you end up after a fall.

Resilience is generally seen as the capacity to overcome trauma, catastrophe, or a debilitating illness. But wait, there's more! It's also an invisible power that fires an internal coping device to fend off the pains of missed deadlines, spilled milk, broken promises, or unmet expectations. This preventive quality is like the Bracelets of Submission Wonder Woman uses to deflect attacks. Think of resilience as your own shield from struggle and a superpower against potential rough conditions.

THE ORIGINS OF RESILIENCE/ RESILIENCE IN CHILDREN

A common picture of childhood resilience is a kid learning to ride a bike. Take my five-year-old friend Colin. It's a tall order for a shorty to figure out how to pedal, balance, steer, and keep an eye on the road all at once. Perseverance and grit fuel him, as it would most kids who want the freedom a bicycle brings. It's a bit simplistic, though, to think that grit equals resilience. While it's part of the overall picture, there's so much more.

We start our lives as resilient, if vulnerable, human beings. While our survival depends on people feeding and caring for us, we are hard-wired to learn, and learning is crucial to resilience. Research has shown, "As we learn something new, cells that send and receive information about the task become more and more efficient. It takes less effort for them to signal the next cell about what's going on. In a sense, the neurons become wired together."[27]

What this means is that while our adult brains are efficiently processing information, we're more creative and adaptive. This is also true for babies. In one study of infants aged five to seven months, researchers noted "that in situations of learning and situations of expectations, babies are in fact able to really quickly use their experience to shift the ways different areas of their brain respond to the environment."[28] Shifting the ways of responding to the environment is a core tenet of resilience, and it's a biological function we've had going for us since we were infants.

The natural tendency to dive right in and learn something new is a quality I find endearing in young children. I'm energized by the uninhibited confidence that propels them into new territory. Research shows that competence and confidence build in children when they are praised for their efforts and encouraged to keep going even when the outcome is unknown.[29] It is this type of encouragement that builds resilience early in a child's development because it cultivates characteristics that are essential to being resilient. Encouragement is an invitation, of sorts, to keep going, dig deeper, and stay curious. Without it, it's common for children to practice risk mitigation by letting someone else lead, anticipating reactions from others before taking action, or, worse, stop trying entirely. Whether explicit or implicit, messages in a child's environment are powerful.

In 1989, developmental psychologist Emmy Werner published the results of her three-decade longitudinal study of six hundred children in Hawaii. She monitored their experiences with family, health, socioeconomic status, and more. Only one-third of the cohort attained adulthood as "competent, confident, and caring adults." Werner discovered that what set these adults apart from the rest of the cohort was their resilience. Some of that resilience was predictive based on preventive factors in their environment. Their own psychology was also integral to their resilience.[30]

Werner discovered that these children possessed what psychologists refer to as a "locus of control." Regardless of their circumstances, they were able to use their skills to deal with life because they saw themselves as the architects of their own achievements. Werner also found that resilience could change over time. While some of the most resilient were overwhelmed by certain stressors, others who were less resilient as children responded more effectively to their circumstances in adulthood.[31] Locus of control is a powerful precursor to and foundation of resilience.

BUILDING RESILIENCE

Martin Seligman is a pioneer in the field of positive psychology, which was first defined and explored by the American psychologist Abraham Maslow. Both Maslow and Seligman have significantly contributed to an ever-expanding body of work focusing on human strengths instead of neuroses. Seligman argues that the most common response to adversity is resilience, not trauma. In his inauguration speech as president of the American Psychological Association in 1998, Seligman said, "The most important thing, the most general thing I learned, was that psychology was half-baked, literally half-baked. We had baked the part about mental illness . . . The other side's unbaked, the side of strength, the side of what we're good at."[32] Seligman's work since then has been grounded in the pursuit of happiness. In *Flourish: A Visionary New Understanding of Happiness and Well-being*, he argues that we're good at learning to regulate our emotions in order to react more positively to negative stimuli.[33]

The basis of Seligman's work is training people to change their "explanatory styles," which are the practices of explaining events to ourselves and others. When people learn to explain events in more external, less internal terms, they experience more positive psychological outcomes and are more resilient. For example:

- **External vs. Internal:** *"This is a bad thing that happened, but I'm not bad, and I did not cause it."*

- **Global vs. Specific:** *"This is something bigger than myself, and my individual actions don't have anything to do with it."*

- **Impermanent vs. Permanent:** *"What's happening now will not always be this way, and I can change my situation."*

Further, resilience wanes when someone views circumstances with exaggerated negativity or dread. As humans, we're all susceptible to what I have long called "optical rectosis," which is my way of making a *shitty outlook* sound like a medical condition. We can make ourselves nuts by catastrophizing and worrying. Then, we're less capable of coping even with the most minor stressors, like being stuck in bumper-to-bumper traffic or spilling coffee. Think about the last time you thought the world was out to get you, and I'll bet you proved it to be true.

Resilience is within reach when we connect to our own locus of control to respond effectively to our environment. For most of us, this doesn't just happen; we have to be intentional with our thoughts and actions to make resilience our default experience. Columbia University clinical psychologist George Bonanno has been studying resilience for nearly thirty years and theorizes about how the way we conceptualize events informs our experience of them.[34] The most resilient people think and act in ways that lead to better outcomes.

Nothing about building resilience is easy or linear; like life, it's messy. But we're not going for perfect. We're going for what's real and moves us forward while doing what must be done: solving problems, attending to our and others' needs, making decisions, influencing or accepting change, communicating, being accountable, and showing up in life. Here are some tools to help build resilience and do all these things, on repeat, without imploding.

FIND MEANING.

Humans are heat-seeking missiles for meaning; constructively interpreting the complex and dynamic world around us takes genuine effort. Because there's so much in the environment for our brains to deal with, we'll readily choose a *flyby* rather than make a landing to do the work. "It will get better" and "Everything happens for a reason" might seem like helpful axioms, but they're actually lies we tell ourselves because randomness is hard to fathom, and sometimes things do get worse. Resilience is forged when we find or make meaning out of what remains.

Years ago, I got a real ego smashing after being laid off from a job I actually hated. In my immediate post-employment *flyby*, I concluded my boss was a jerk who didn't appreciate my brilliance. In reality, he laid off many competent people because the company was in dire straits financially. (It ultimately went bankrupt.) You might have missed that *I hated the job.* After I wallowed for weeks, a trusted friend asked me if this wasn't a victory since I had been delivered from misery. There, within the ruins of my battered ego, was an opportunity to find empowering meaning in the loss. It wasn't hard to see that once I looked closely, but I'd gotten caught up in the trappings of the job—an SVP title, a big salary, the corner office—and lost sight of my professional values. Since then, I've only chosen work I find engaging, team-oriented, and focused on improving the lives of others.

LOOK FOR THE GOOD STUFF.

In the organizational development field, "appreciative inquiry" is the practice of identifying strengths and what's best in the world around us. Noble, right? Yet, because we're more skilled at noticing glitches than glories, the practice requires us to exercise a commonly atrophied cognitive muscle. Just check your daily news feed for proof that calamity captivates most of our attention. Owing to evolution and the drive to survive, our brain scans for threats, and when it finds them, our central nervous system activates with an energizing bang of adrenaline and cortisol.

Good news, on the other hand, might elicit an audible, "Awwwwww, that's sweet," but . . . meh. Resilience may not be exciting, but it's a long game that pays off when we slow down, summon our superpowers, and ask questions like:

- What or who is thriving here and why?
- What's happening that produces good stuff, and how can I get more of that?
- What are the useful, helpful, or productive actions other people are taking?

We don't need to possess gushing positivity to see the bright side. We just have to bother to look.

BE VULNERABLE.

By all accounts, Dr. Brené Brown has changed the way people view vulnerability. She's shown us, through deep research and personal stories, that vulnerability equals courage. There are heaps of desired leadership characteristics, but none as important as courage. It takes courage to make tough decisions in the face of mounting evidence that you're going to piss someone off. We can do hard things, but hoo-boy! Hard things are hard.

In a world that treasures expertise and confidence, who wants to confess ignorance, doubts, or faults?

My given last name is Rice, which a colleague once told me I should change to "Right" because being wrong was anathema to me. (No surprise, this was difficult to admit.) When we're vulnerable, we make way for others' vulnerability. Remove pretense and emotional armor by admitting mistakes, copping to weaknesses, and exposing scars. Nothing about it may feel comfortable at first, but that's proof you're doing it right.

FORM A TRIBE.

Tribe. Support system. Posse. Human social group. Circle. Whatever you call it, get thee one. We're hard-wired for connection, and history proves our survival is rooted in sharing, trading, and reciprocating. Feelings of connection with others are linked to the hormone oxytocin, the "feel-good" chemical. When your body gets a good dose of oxytocin, you're less anxious, which helps you think more clearly and make better decisions. Any social circle in which you feel affirmed and understood is likely to spark your oxytocin. Circles like neighborhood groups, religious communities, book clubs, professional affiliations, clubs, or schools, to name a few, are great sources of companionship with like-minded people. These are the people with whom you might share dreams, fears, hopes, troubles, and, if you're very lucky, some raucous laughter. It's plausible they'll help you do other resilience work as well, like asking for help, spotting what's positive, and making meaning.

EXERCISE.

My love affair with exercise is on-again, off-again in spite of the evidence linking physical and mental health. Mostly I just hike and dance, both of which achieve the goal of a brain that oozes mood-altering endorphins, dopamine, and serotonin. Exercise is also proven to mitigate the effects of cortisol[35] (the stress hormone), which, if allowed to run free, damages your hippocampus, the place where the brain consolidates information for memory and spatial orientation.[36] All in all, your brain works better when it's running on exercise. And when your brain is working better, you're better at doing hard things—like being resilient.

BEWARE KRYPTONITE

You probably know about kryptonite. It's the fictional green, red, or gold substance in the Superman stories that creates different reactions in the titular hero that ultimately reveal an "exploitable weakness." On our own hero's journey, we might encounter a similar variety of forces bent on our destruction.

The first is *gaslighting,* a form of psychological manipulation to sow doubt in memory, perception, or judgment. Gaslighting occurs when someone continually challenges your reality or pressures you to question your beliefs or attitudes. We can also gaslight ourselves by second-guessing our decisions, shaming ourselves for making mistakes, or waving off our accomplishments as "dumb luck." The result can be stunted self-esteem, low confidence, and the inability to see our beautiful selves.

The second force is *unrelenting stress or chaos.* Our bodies' stress response is designed to keep us alive; consider the built-in mechanisms of fight, flight, or freeze. We are not, however, meant to live in a constant state of stress, which, if left unchecked, can lead to a depressed immune system, heart disease, or other medical issues.[37] Energy diverted toward fighting fear is energy we can't deploy to find healing.

The third force against resilience is one where I personally excel: *taking myself (or others) too seriously.* I can make a federal case out of the most minor infraction, particularly when stressed. I'm more likely to give myself grace than offer it to others, judging their actions as abominable while viewing my own mistakes as good intentions gone awry. In either case, a lighter touch is better. Too much seriousness zaps our capacity to see the best in others and envision a brighter future.

A LEADER'S TOOLBELT FOR CREATING A CULTURE OF RESILIENCE

I n my humble opinion, resilience is a defining characteristic of effective leadership. When leaders demonstrate resilience, they model what it means to be human in the face of challenge. Cultivating resilience is a way of unleashing potential, which in turn helps create a supportive workplace.

Let's unpack **U.N.L.E.A.S.H.**:

Undo practices and policies that no longer work. Sacred cows are loitering in plain sight, criticized in private but protected in public for fear of offending the creator (which might, in fact, be you!): the weekly status-update meeting that's turned into a "show and tell" or that report a few people spend precious time preparing, but no one reads. Everyone can see they don't serve the common good. These bovines take up precious time, space, and energy. As a leader who knows your team's energy is finite and must be conserved to handle crises, it's up to you to call the audible. Have courage, and do the thing that must be done.

Nurture creativity. Transforming ideas into reality boosts confidence and resilience because it demonstrates that something once unimaginable is possible. Creativity requires involvement and interest, which can make us feel like we are living fully.

Welcome multiple perspectives, invite questions, stay curious, and shake off the missteps. When you demonstrate an open mind, you give others permission to try something new when they might have otherwise played it safe.

Learn new ways to respond to the environment. Shifting, adapting, or pivoting to a changing workplace has never been more critical than it is in the digital age. Agility is the name of the game, and education is the way to stay a player. Resilient leaders are open to learning about both their strengths and their limitations. They're also willing to adopt different methods to operate and administrate, even when current efforts have been successful. Sometimes, it's just time to change things up.

Envision a better future. A leader with a positive vision for the future inspires and engages. Look for what could be better, even if things are going just fine—but especially if they aren't. There's nothing more dispiriting than requiring a team to slog through challenges without a sense that their efforts will yield meaningful or lasting results. Worthwhile things aren't always easy; they aren't supposed to be. That's why it's especially important to create a powerful and positive vision.

Admit the shank. Nobody's perfect, and it's a real relief when our leaders and those we admire demonstrate fallibility. It's likely obvious when a leader swings and misses, so admission of your mistake isn't typically revelatory. Rather, it's a way to deepen trust in the team by demonstrating humility and maintaining a grip on reality.

Show up. Both good and bad days come with the territory, so there's no sense pretending otherwise. Start where you are, and do your best. Give yourself and others grace. Tomorrow is a chance for a fresh start.

Help others gain agency. Some of us have a larger locus of control in the workplace than others. That's the reality—not everyone can be in charge. But we all like to have at least a sense of control and know we're making a difference, either as an individual or as part of a team. Unleashing a team's potential requires leaders to deliver tools, guidance, and space for people to grow. When possible, let people set their own goals, make their own decisions, and assess their own outcomes.

ADDITIONAL INSIGHT FROM THE LAB

There is no shortage of source material on resilience, and I wrestled with who to reference as I wrote this chapter. In addition to those I've already mentioned, I was particularly moved by the story and work of therapist Michael Kalous. In a 2017 TED Talk, he explained his work with children who have lived through severe trauma and generously shared his own painful experience. Whether or not children are raised under stressed or traumatic circumstances, there are some very specific protective factors that promote resilience and help children grow up well-adjusted. Sometimes these factors are cultivated by children themselves, either consciously or subconsciously. Sometimes they are promoted in the culture around them through the media, religious or spiritual communities, and society at large. These are the factors Kalous attributes to resilience, including his own:[38]

- **Having someone to look up to:** a hero.

- **Having a place to escape:** a safe haven or refuge.

- **Having solitude:** a place to find some peace and quiet.

- **Having agency:** being able to control something, anything.

- **Having purpose:** recognizing the meaning in things.

In my mind's eye, I easily revisit my own childhood, where I searched for any people, places, and purpose to make me feel as though I belonged. The need for belonging is a natural state and follows each of us into adulthood.

Our psychological well-being, whether as children or adults, is at the root of our ability to overcome challenges and thrive.

Research on human development is rich with the specific environmental and social conditions that are integral to emotional health. Some of the most fascinating research I came upon was from psychologist Urie Bronfenbrenner. Bronfenbrenner developed what is commonly referred to as the ecological/systems framework that identifies the environment in which individuals interact. This is important because it influences our development as children and informs our ability as adults to cope with crises and display commonly understood characteristics of resilience. Bronfenbrenner defined five separate but interrelated systems that define the values and norms that shape psychological development:[39]

- **Micro-system:** The family, peer, religious, health, and education system into which we were born.

- **Meso-system:** The interrelationship and interdependencies of the systems into which we were born.

- **Exo-system:** The relationship between a child and the experiences of parent/parent-like figures, which may include things like moving for a job, adult conflict, divorce, and the like.

- **Macro-system:** The overarching culture influencing a child's development, including (but not necessarily limited to) geography, socioeconomic status, and ethnicity.

- **Chrono-system:** The pattern of environmental events and transitions over the course of life.

To state the obvious, we're influenced by the systems (ecology) around us, and our psychological development has been inextricably linked to that ecology. You, me, us . . . we're going to come to the world enveloped in these environmental influences. The way we grow up has a lot to do with the way we show up as adults. And, yet, as adults, while we may be shaped by these influences, we can shake them and reshape ourselves to not just live but thrive. The superpower of resilience, perhaps lost to us through life's trials, can be reclaimed by creating our own healthy environments.

KEEP GOING: CONCLUSION

Each of us has a story, and some measure of resilience is likely central to our personal narratives. What I discovered while researching and writing this chapter is that although life can be brutal, resilience is possible. Whether captured in sociologists' discoveries or revealed in psychologists' research, there's powerful evidence that we can be resilient in the face of trauma and stress. While resilience might be a reflex for some people, for most of us, it's a learned choice. The stories about the people in my life, and my own story, have shown me there is every reason to choose resilience every day.

43

* * * * *

CHAPTER THREE

AUTHENTICITY

Clark Kent is an eager, awkward newspaper reporter; Bruce Wayne a troubled, discreet playboy; and Peter Parker a lonely, earnest student. These identities mask a truer version of these characters, a version so powerful that most of the time, they hide it. Yet when they do step into the power of their superhero selves, the world benefits from their courage, strength, and desire to do good.

Although we don't don shiny outfits, scale tall buildings, and pull back cars careening off cliffs, it's likely each of us has a deeper, truer version of ourselves, in which we can feel like and be perceived as our best, most potent selves.

The stories of most superheroes include wrestling with their authenticity, contending with the messiness of their fear, anger, courage, and goodness. When they embrace all of it, the fullness of their authentic selves, they access powers that change the world.

AUTHENTICITY AND CHILDREN

If you want to see the full range of human behavior, head to a playground. There, we can watch with alarm as kids hit and scream to stay in possession of what is "*Mine!*" We delight as they laugh with abandon and create imaginary worlds unknown by grown-ups. One thing we can count on is that what we see is what we get. We know which child is angry, which one is a risk-taker, and which one is feeling shy or betrayed. Children are authentic because they have not yet learned to be anything else.

Recently, I was out with my three-year-old niece and her grandmother, whom she calls Grammy, after getting ice cream cones. When two women approached us carrying their own cones, my niece ran up to them and shouted with delight, "Hi! I just had ice cream too! What kind of ice cream are you eating?!"

They laughed, "We're having chocolate chip."

"Oh, that sounds yummy! I had raspberry-lemon. It was delicious!"

"It sounds delicious!" they said as they smiled and continued walking.

My niece plopped herself back in front of them. "My name is Adeline. What are your names?" The younger woman responded with her name, and then Adeline pointed her finger at the older woman, "And what's your name?"

"My name is Grammy. I'm her Grammy."

"What?!" Adeline shouted. She threw her hands in the air, her little body shaking with excitement, pointed to her grandmother, and exclaimed, "Her name is Grammy too! You guys are twins!"

With four grown-ups bent over with laughter in the middle of the sidewalk, Adeline sensed she had a captivated audience and proclaimed, "Now that I've had ice cream, I'm going to do some exercises!" As she furiously demonstrated a series of toe touches, we adults delighted at a three-year-old embracing her curiosity and being entirely herself.

A favorite thing about young children is how utterly themselves they are. They have no sophisticated filters for their behaviors.

They are new to their impulses, feelings, and how they affect the people around them, and they haven't yet mastered reading a situation and making modifications to suit it. Adeline wanted to talk to strangers about ice cream and keep their attention. She used the power of her unfiltered, authentic personality to do just that.

Of course, children's authenticity is not always so delightful. Most of us have cringed at a child's unfiltered observations. Adeline once shouted to a man with pockmarked skin, "What happened to your face?" The frustration, jealousy, and exhaustion we suppress as adults are often on full display in children. There have been many uncomfortable situations when some kid was screaming his head off, and I thought, "Yup, me too, buddy, me too."

The world's response to children is part of what shapes their developing authenticity. The rules of life will be taught to them in a variety of ways, and their behavioral filters will follow. As they learn what is appropriate to share and what is better left unsaid, they'll develop techniques to help them stay likable, accepted, and even safe. They'll soften to protect others and harden to protect themselves. And so, the distance will grow between what they genuinely think and feel and what they actually do and say.

WHY AUTHENTICITY IS A SUPERPOWER

R esearch indicates that authenticity is linked to our sense of well-being, autonomy, and ability to experience the best aspects of our personalities.[40] We *feel* better and more in control when we are authentic. Unsurprisingly, authenticity is also linked to better-quality relationships.

We seek authentic others because they usually exhibit admirable ease and comfort with themselves. We feel that what we see is what we get, which makes it easier to trust them. Even if we are unsure whether we like someone, at least we feel more certain of whom we are dealing with. Trust is at the heart of relationship building, and authenticity is at the heart of trust.

Perhaps the most important aspect of this superpower is that it's contagious, which may be why so many of us love being with children. As we get older, it can feel risky to expose our truest, more vulnerable selves. Yet when we do, we demonstrate the courage to show up more honestly and freely. We inspire others to consider traits and preferences they may be hiding or cultural norms of which they're unaware. As we reveal more of ourselves, we invite others to do the same.

One way I capitalize on the contagious nature of this superpower is to bust through those polite, boring cocktail conversations we've all suffered through. I turn the topic from traffic or some-body's beach vacation to a light-hearted, truthful reveal of some current fear or anxiety I'm battling. After a flicker of surprise, I usually see relief cross people's faces as they realize, "Oh, we're going to talk about how we *really* feel!" Bodies relax, and the conversation takes off with renewed energy as it becomes more vulnerable and real.

AUTHENTICITY AND GROWN-UPS

To be effective in the world, we modify our behaviors for different people and places. If we feel happiest and most authentic taking charge of a conversation or strutting our musical theater moves, that's great to know—but we can't do these things *all* the time. Sometimes my boss or client is going to insist on taking control of the conversation—I need to let them. It simply won't serve me to dance the grapevine while interviewing for the paralegal gig I want. Luckily, the range of our authenticity can expand far beyond our greatest affinities and comfort areas.

As Walt Whitman said, "I am large, I contain multitudes."[41] Most of us are larger and contain more multitudes than we think! We make natural adjustments for others all the time without even thinking about it. We behave a little differently with our friends than with our parents, and this may vary from how we are with colleagues or a romantic partner. Usually, as we adjust to these different roles, we remain genuine and true to ourselves. In different situations, we access different parts of ourselves, sometimes turning the volume up on one characteristic and down on another. I used to adore spending time with my grandparents. I also loved partying in the woods with my friends. I behaved very differently in each setting but was happily authentic in both.

A few years ago, I ran regular workshops at a prestigious financial services firm in Manhattan, where, to meet their expectations of formality, I focused on my poise and articulation while dressed in my slickest business attire. I was also engaged in a weekly coaching job for a hip media firm in Brooklyn, where one of the partners teased me about my "fancy blazer," and they greatly appreciated the use of a well-placed curse word. I was doing similar work for both places but modified my behaviors and style so that my work would resonate with each culture.

Question: how can we know if adjustments we make for others diminish our authenticity? Answer: we play around with what feels right. Remember, playfulness is one of our superpowers! Ask yourself: Am I modifying my behavior so I can have a greater impact, or so I can put others at ease? Am I communicating differently so I can be better understood to create more connection? We can certainly adjust for these reasons without sacrificing core beliefs and qualities. (Such investments could be considered emotional intelligence, an important, related capability.) But if we reflexively change the way we speak and react in order to gain acceptance, constantly worrying about saying the "right" things, we diminish our ability both to feel and be perceived as authentic. If the adjustments we make for others become exhausting or unsettling, that may indicate a relationship or situation isn't right for us.

Common barriers to authenticity are:

- Our own comfort and confidence in who we are and what we have to offer.

- Messages from the environment about its acceptance of us.

AUTHENTICITY AND CONFIDENCE

One thing that helped me maintain my authenticity in those two diverse settings was my belief in the work I was there to do and my ability to do it. I could hold onto my values and use my skills while maintaining my sense of self—whether I was talking to poised people in designer suits or lounging on a conference room sofa with folks in fleece jackets. I actually enjoyed flexing for them because even if they challenged my ideas, it was clear my clients were respectfully challenging *ideas*, not *me* or my right to be there.

Had I been less sure of myself, my flexing would have been more stressful than fun. I'd have been more intent on fitting in, proving my value, and playing it safe so as not to offend. We rarely shine when our objective is to avoid offense. Playing it safe makes us smaller.

Authenticity is harder when we feel insecure or unsure of ourselves. I know two sisters who exemplify the contrast between insecurity and confidence and how both can impact our authenticity. One sister suffers from social anxiety. She doesn't trust people's motives and deeply worries about what people think of her. She struggles with authenticity because her own sense of self is unstable; she seems to understand herself mostly through the lens of others. (Many of us can relate to this, especially in the age of social media.) It's hard to believe you can be yourself when you're unsure who that self is. When talking about authenticity, remember that we don't all start from the same place. "Just be yourself" requires an effort for some that those with higher self-esteem may not appreciate.

Her confident sister conveys more authenticity because she has a secure sense of who she is. She trusts her own instincts and tells it as she sees it, so you always know where she stands. High confidence, however, can also inhibit authenticity. She sometimes hides behind her confidence, erecting a wall of self-assurance. You hope she'll open a window in that wall, both so she'll better see you and so you can better see her.

Authenticity isn't a steady state. Some days we feel braver, allowing more windows, and some days we fortify our walls. As we explore who we are and how to present our truest (most potent!) selves, either too little or too much confidence can present obstacles.

AUTHENTICITY AND OUR ENVIRONMENT

My authenticity stayed intact while in those differing work cultures, but the truth is, I wasn't sure this was sustainable. Shortly before I'd left one position, I started to feel like I wasn't just flexing; I was pretending. We all know the only way to be accepted by certain people and places is to pretend to think, feel, and behave as they do. We might act like we think something is funny, excuse behavior we don't like, or withhold opinions. Most of us expect to have to do this from time to time.

The world is wide, and sometimes we will feel like "a fish out of water." But many people struggle when the place they have to function feels restrictively misaligned with how they prefer to behave and present themselves.

As a coach, I work with folks who want to be better at flexing their behaviors and skills so they can be more effective at work. As they try new things, we track their comfort level. They stretch out of their current comfort zones and challenge their risk tolerance; this is good! Again, we are large; we contain multitudes. Discovering the range of our authenticity requires exploring the breadth and depth of those multitudes. If we want to thrive, we mustn't get stuck in narrow definitions of who we are; we have to play around with the edges of what is comfortable and how we do things. I can't overestimate the value of emulating the playfulness of children when stretching into the full spectrum of our authenticity.

However, we shouldn't feel pressure to stretch away from what's comfortable for the purpose of feeling accepted, valued, and heard. If we consistently have to change our behaviors to gain belonging and acceptance, our authenticity and sense of self will unravel. It's impossible to talk about authenticity without acknowledging the role of bias in many cultures.

Rules and norms of cultures vary in transparency and subtlety. Sometimes the rules we have to flex to are informed by unconscious preferences and bias. Women and people of color can be especially taxed when flexing to their environments because subtle norms are informed by so much that is masculine and white-centered.

No matter how good we may be at flexing, some situations make authenticity feel impossible. To be seen as our true selves, we first must be seen. Here's a scenario I have heard countless times from black and female colleagues: They make a comment or suggestion that maybe earns a head nod, but more often goes without a response. Moments later, a white and/or male colleague says the *same* thing, and it's readily acknowledged and discussed. To compound the problem further, their attempts to call out the situation are usually ignored or invalidated. When we experience this kind of rejection or barrier to being seen and heard, authenticity is simply not viable.

Creating inclusive environments means building a space in which *everyone* feels they have the opportunity to thrive. Inclusiveness is acceptance and validation of many ways of doing and being, enabling *all* people to safely explore the full range of their authenticity.

AUTHENTICITY AND PERCEPTION

The world is filled with people who appear calm and confident on the outside but are shaking in their boots on the inside. So yeah, we can successfully appear authentic without feeling it. But this is exhausting and usually not sustainable. All my clients want alternatives to the "fake it 'til you make it" strategy. And none of my clients experiencing imposter syndrome is having a good time, even if they are excellent imposters.

On the flip side, someone who *feels* authentic might not be *perceived* that way. When we gauge our impact on others, it's good to remember that even if we flex and adjust our style, sometimes we just won't get each other. This is one of the reasons that authenticity serves us so well: seeing who responds to us when we are fully ourselves is how we find our people, those who accept, honor, and value us for the qualities that make us feel the most comfortable, content, alive, and at ease.

CONCLUSION: AUTHENTICITY IS COMPLICATED FOR ADULTS

Adeline's "What happened to your face?" comment and our discussion of the need to adapt to others show us what's difficult about authenticity. In its purest form, authenticity doesn't always serve us. Those raw playground behaviors can fill us with delight but also horror. Bruce Banner is effective as both a quiet scientist and the Hulk, but he needs some degree of control over his various impulses for his superpower to do good rather than harm.

To be an adult striving for authenticity requires the courage to show up in the world as you are alongside a willingness to meet that world as it is. It may reject your big ideas and your strange jokes, but you have options!

You can keep telling your strange jokes until you meet the people who love them. Or, if you can't find enough of those people, you can repackage the truths that fuel your big ideas and jokes so that more people can hear you. A willingness to stay connected to your truths while *also* playing around with how you express them will harness the superpower of your authenticity. Authenticity is a journey. It's a lifelong exercise to benefit from the unique collection of traits, emotions, experiences, and expressions that are the one and only you.

AUTHENTICITY AND LEADERSHIP: A LEADERSHIP TOOLBELT (G.U.T.S.)

In my work, I see three core reasons people need their leaders' authenticity:

AUTHENTICITY BEGETS AUTHENTICITY.

We've explored the numerous reasons authenticity is a super-power: heightened well-being, better relationships, and access to our best and most potent selves. When we see our leaders as authentic, we feel permission to be the same. We get braver, reveal more to each other, and create a space where more people can access the potential of their full selves. When we feel like we have to play small or bend ourselves to fit in, we are not doing our best work. We suffer, and that, too, is contagious. An authentic leader promotes an authentic, flourishing culture of diverse voices and shared well-being.

G—As you explore the behaviors to embody as a leader, make sure they feel consistent with who you are in the other roles in your life. If something feels unnatural or inauthentic to you, chances are it appears the same to others. Trust the influence of **genuine connection** and a communication style that demonstrates ease as much as command.

U—**Unloose** a variety of ideas and styles around you by encouraging multiple perspectives and ways of contributing.

TRUST IS AT THE FOUNDATION OF SUCCESSFUL LEADERSHIP.

We take more risks, dig deeper, and go the extra mile for people we trust. A leader who is overly polished, polite, or perfect makes most of us uneasy. We wonder what's really going on beneath that carefully managed outer layer. An authentic leader builds trust because people believe they are getting the full and true picture of who that leader is—a person responsible for both their strengths and weaknesses. We have the sense that because this leader admits flaws and shares hard truths, we are getting more information, which puts us on more solid ground and enables us to make better decisions. When leaders are authentic, they demonstrate their trust in us as well. It's as if they're saying, "I trust you with the complexity of who I am and the hard truths we will have to navigate together."

T—Show people you **trust** them enough to reveal both the person who can do your job successfully and the person who will get it wrong sometimes. Let people in on the questions you are asking and the things you wonder about as you make the big decisions. Transparency into your thinking and feeling doesn't undermine your authority; it shows people how and why you've earned it.

PEOPLE NEED TO SEE A POSSIBLE VERSION OF THEMSELVES IN THEIR LEADERS.

I am in awe of the number of individuals who struggle in their organizations without a role model to look up to. They can't envision themselves in a leadership role because their leaders seem distant and unrelatable, which is usually connected to feeling that their leadership lacks authenticity and transparency into who they really are. People want examples of how leaders balance their professional and personal lives. Being singularly work- and results-focused seems daunting and undesirable. They need to see leaders who connect in authentic ways, who can be vulnerable, and who don't put on a show of having every-thing figured out.

S—To the extent you are comfortable, **share stories** about your personal life. To believe we can keep our personal and professional lives separate is naïve. The stories we consume and the tabloids we buy feed our insatiable curiosity about the personal lives of public figures, which carries over to the people who influence our daily lives: our leaders. Show your willingness to be known beyond your function and get curious about who others are beyond theirs. If this kind of openness isn't authentic to you, explain to them why you might appear closed. Let them see it's a choice to be private, not a mandate. You don't have to gladhand and schmooze, but you do need to make an effort to connect. To build trust, demonstrate a desire to be seen and to see those around you. Share what motivates and matters to you. In doing this, you stretch out a hand to those looking up at you. You show them that to lead here is not to diminish your other facets but to step more bravely into the fullness of who you are.

ADDITIONAL INSIGHT
FROM THE LAB

"Studies of individual differences in authenticity show that people who are generally more authentic—more autonomous and genuine—have greater well-being."[42] Autonomy is one of our basic psychological needs and, as Ryan and Ryan explain, is "definitional to authenticity."

In her paper, "Authenticity in Context: Being True to Working Selves," Serena Chen asserts that "alongside global forms of self-conceptions and self-knowledge, people have multiple, context-specific selves, with different selves brought to the foreground in different contexts."[43]

Satisfaction in various roles is related to the way we experience the Big Five personality traits, which are considered relatively consistent. People who reported feeling more "authentic" in their roles felt more openness, extraversion, agreeableness, and conscientiousness, and less neuroticism.[44]

Research and literature discuss authenticity in a wide variety of ways, fundamentally all related to the Oxford English Dictionary definition: the quality of being genuine or true.[45]

·····

CHAPTER FOUR

COMPASSION

MEET MARCUS

Before entering business, I was an elementary school teacher. In one of my classes, I had a student—let's call him Marcus. Marcus was ten years old, almost average height, wire-thin, and wore oversized glasses. He was well-spoken and had a broad vocabulary. But above all, Marcus was a challenge for any teacher.

He could disrupt, distract, or divide the group at will. There were days when he would poke at other members of our classroom just to set them off, diverting my attention and derailing the lesson. He slammed his books, threw chairs, and started arguments.

What was interesting about this situation was that the other students weren't chomping at the bit to imitate Marcus, but they didn't shun him either. He was still included in conversations, still allowed to sit with them at the lunch table, and still invited to play at recess. Once he was disciplined, the kids just let it go.

Most of the children felt for Marcus. They most likely did not fully understand his situation, but they had compassion. They ascribed no judgment to his behavior—they accepted him. Marcus was a frequent flyer at the Discipline Office, but whenever his mother needed to be involved, he would cry. On one occasion, he threw a book that accidentally hit another student in the head. After the Dean called his mother, Marcus came back to class and sobbed quietly. The student he hit with the book comforted him. I remember her saying, "I know you didn't mean to—tell your mom it was an accident." They worried after Marcus—more concerned with his well-being than the repercussions of his behavior.

The same could not be said for the teachers. Many of the teachers felt Marcus was beyond help—a troubled child who was incapable of correcting course. Over a number of years, his behavior had gotten worse and worse. With his broad vocabulary and "bookish" looks, he was clearly just "acting up." The collective adult wisdom that was passed from teacher to teacher was that Marcus was not a child to be taught but to be endured. Just get him to the next grade.

When I got my class assignment, these teachers came to warn me. In varied conversations, I got the same message: Marcus was brilliant, bored, and troublesome. Beware.

By midyear, I had also made no progress in figuring out how to help—and I could feel my own frustration building. Then, I realized that none of the kids were frustrated by him—and I was so perplexed. He commanded so much attention, yet no one faulted him for it. They treated him with such compassion. I needed to be more like them. I thought about his family situation, the school system, and its culture and found much to be concerned about. I did make an attempt to apply everything I knew to do: new books, new desk location, more free time, less free time—all trying to treat the symptoms Marcus was showing.

I knew his behaviors were a symptom of someone in distress and not the definition of who he could be. Revisiting what I actually knew about Marcus—what I had seen with my own eyes—I came to understand that his behavior was driven by a need to hide from the reality that he had been promoted year after year without having done the work. Marcus had fallen behind. I was on the road of compassion.

Now we had a plan of attack—real action that we could take. He worked with a number of resources and began to make meaningful progress. By year's end, Marcus's trips to the Discipline Office had tapered off. He made meaningful progress in closing the gap with his peers. Best of all, I would see him the following year in the hallway smiling, talking with friends, and acting joyful. The same kids who never thumbed their noses at Marcus—who had always shown compassion. Finally, Marcus could be himself.

Marcus's story is exemplary of childhood compassion, but it is not an exceptional story. In my teaching career, the behavior of Marcus's classmates was the rule—not the exception.

WHAT IS COMPASSION?

What is compassion? A definition may not come quickly since it is often an attribute that gets conflated with other attributes. It is also a word that we may more viscerally understand. Simply, it may be the one lost superpower that we recognize immediately when we see it in action.

When I'm talking about compassion, I'm referring to the ability to recognize distress, suffering, or an unmet need in others without judgment and take considered action to alleviate the distress.

Compassion, empathy, and sympathy are often conflated. Let's dissect them and provide some clarity.

First, empathy is about connecting to all sorts of emotional feelings and expressions, including amusement, pride, anger, and sorrow, to name a few. Essentially, being able to see someone else's experience and imagine yourself in their place. Compassion is targeted specifically at suffering, recognizing when others are in pain and acting upon it.

Imagine (insert your favorite superhero here) looking down on an apartment building with great empathy. The dastardly villain, Mr. Freeze, is planning to freeze the building and all of its occupants. The empathetic superhero would immediately comprehend the dangers the people are in, how they may feel cold at first, and then warm, and then, well, dead. The superhero may let them know that the hero understands their condition since the hero has been frozen before.

For the building's occupants, all of this empathy is just not enough. What they want is action. Surely our superhero could use compassion here not only to empathize but to throw down their supershield to protect the inhabitants. While there is a risk to our superhero—perhaps the villain has a countershield—the hero takes action. It is what superheroes do.

The relationship between empathy and compassion is similar to the riddle, "In a bacon and egg breakfast, what's the difference between the chicken and the pig? The chicken is involved, but the pig is committed." Empathy is clearly involved, but compassion is committed. It is worthwhile noting that in the *Super Chicken* cartoon, Super Chicken is both involved and committed.

Second, while empathy can be a catalyst for compassion, it is clearly not required and not the endgame. For example, imagine an adult comforting a child who is terrified of a small, barking dog. The adult doesn't need to feel the child's fear to help. There can be compassion for the child, a desire to make his or her distress go away, without any shared experience or empathetic effort. Empathy does have compelling value, though, since being more empathetic increases our awareness of those around us.

Sympathy is also confused with compassion. Sympathy may not be abundant in adults, but children six and younger offer it extremely well—when another student fails a test or struggles to read, they don't tease them or say, "Wow, guess you didn't work hard enough." They just try to comfort the other in pain.

Sympathy falls short, though, because it again refers to feeling bad for others without the impulse for action. You may feel sympathy for a friend who fell and broke his ankle, but it is not compassion until you help them shovel their walk or take their garbage out.

Compassion involves feeling emotions that are more appropriate to another's situation than to one's own (empathy), along with elements of condolence, pity, and/or agreement (sympathy), resulting in the act of help or support for another.

Compassion is NOT self-serving. Chinese philosopher Mencius described it in this way: "Suppose someone suddenly saw a child about to fall into a well: anyone in such a situation would have a feeling of alarm and compassion—not because one sought to get in good with the child's parents, not because one wanted fame among one's neighbors and friends, and not because one would dislike the sound of the child's cries. From this, we can see that if one is without the feeling of compassion, one is not human."[46]

All major modern religions venerate compassion. The veneration is driven in part from the reality that the individual is taking action to alleviate someone else's pain—without the expectation of reciprocity. This action can also be filled with personal risk since none of us have a Vibranium shield.

When we witness compassion—the person who donates a kidney, saves a family from a burning home, or helps a struggling colleague—it gives us pause. It is the action that captures both our attention and our admiration.

THE COMPASSIONATE CHILD

P sychology once held that human beings are born as blank slates—*tabula rasa*—to be inscribed with knowledge through life's experience. But we know better now. We are not blank slates and never were. Research has shown that there are strong genetic influences on a vast array of personal characteristics. Most importantly, certain elements of being are not genetic—but universally human.

We are wired to be social. Newborns, hours after birth, express the desire to socialize—and prefer the sight of a human face to any other object.[47] In twin studies, fetuses begin to interact with each other as early as the fourteenth week.[48] Before we're even born, we are wired to connect with others.

Being built to interact with others, we are born with a sense of compassion. Psychologist Dr. Paul Bloom asserts, "Once they're capable of coordinated movement, babies will often try to soothe others who are suffering by patting and stroking."[49] Toddlers as young as eighteen months old understand when others need help and will often take some sort of action as a response.[50] They act without reward or praise for their behavior—it comes from a genuine desire to heal the hurting of another. In fact, some researchers have identified a state of euphoria known as "helper's high," or feeling happy because you helped others.[51] Your brain wants you to feel good about helping others. What an amazing superpower.

The acts that develop from compassion evolve as children age. Infants display an innate understanding of others' emotions; for example, they may cry when others are crying. Two-year-olds may go to their own caregiver to comfort a friend, while just a couple of years later, they know that their friend needs their own caregiver. This big transition happens at roughly age four when we begin to understand other people have separate bodies, experiences, knowledge, and feelings.

Imagine you're three, sitting in preschool. The teacher sends a classmate out of the room and then shows you a candy box. You think, "Candy, yes," but the opened box reveals pennies. When she calls the classmate back into the room and asks you what they will think is in the now-closed candy box, you proudly announce, "Pennies," unaware that your classmate does not know what you know.

Once you enter kindergarten, you are now wise to the world and would most likely answer "Candy!" This false-belief task identifies perspective-taking—the ability to separate our experience from the experience of others. This is the empathetic mind at work.

Cognitive components of developed compassion typically come together by age six or seven, when a child is more capable of taking another person's perspective and offering solutions or help to someone in distress.

This ability to take someone else's perspective is invaluable for leaders. It allows them, should they access it, the ability to consider how best to communicate, establish goals, and make decisions. Ultimately, it is their level of compassion that determines how they actually lead.

WHERE DID THE COMPASSION GO?

So, humans are born compassionate, and it grows as we grow. Then what happens?

Middle school. Several studies have shown that compassion declined significantly as students transitioned from the fourth to sixth grades.[52] Thinking about childhood development, this shift corresponds with children establishing their identities, social circles, and hierarchies. Our ability (and speed) to see patterns and categorize begins to crowd out our innate ability to be compassionate.

This is when the "us versus other" thinking starts to accelerate. Our brains are wired to make quick sense of a complex world. Labeling people and putting them in boxes is an inelegant response. While we may have great compassion for "us," those "others" are getting what they most likely deserve. When we begin to see people as "other," we question their actions and have a support network to justify our inaction.

As an objective trait, compassion is considered primarily positive. As a subjective experience, compassion can involve both negative and positive emotions. The complication is that perceiving others' suffering can lead to less noble states, like personal distress, anger, or even righteous satisfaction. As we grow older, the downside of being compassionate begins to emerge in our thinking. Compassion takes on an even more cognitive quality.

Even if we acknowledge the pain of the "others," acting with compassion can be risky. As I mentioned before, compassion starts to fade as social circles and hierarchies are etched into our minds. Straying from those circles—like being compassionate to someone outside the circle—can cause you to lose social standing. There can be a real physical risk of taking action. We also face the reality that the action itself may not resolve the pain—potentially leading to guilt or survivor's remorse.

Finally, many of us also become led to believe that our evolution is due to natural selection and the *"survival of the fittest"*—a phrase often attributed to Charles Darwin's work on evolution. This aligns with the clichés that it is a "dog-eat-dog world" so "kill or be killed" because life is "every man for himself." Darwin, however, would disagree with this adulterated view of his work.

Darwin's theory of natural selection is really not about the warrior culture winning but the more adaptive one. What is far less celebrated from Darwin are his findings in *The Descent of Man*. Here, Darwin notes that "those communities which included the greatest number of sympathetic members would flourish best, and rear the greatest number of offspring."[53] Darwin believed that societies that support one another and demonstrate compassion are best poised for survival.

THE SUCCESS-COMPASSION PARADOX

As our "social status" improves, our compassion and interest in perspective-seeking can diminish. The mentalizer's paradox is the belief that thinking about how others think and feel is for lower-status individuals. Simply, the higher people rise in terms of status, the less they feel the need to think about others—and the more they believe others should think about them. After all, they are higher on the food chain!

One of the leaders at my first company mentioned to me that I should join a country club. While he knew my salary (low) and family situation (three children), and in fact, shared my situation when he was younger, he had lost perspective. What he was suggesting was without merit for my situation.

But why would wealth and status decrease our feelings of compassion for others? Logic would suggest that having few resources would lead to selfishness. This is not the case. Researchers suspect that the answer may have something to do with how wealth and abundance give us a sense of freedom and independence from others. Simply, the better off we are, the more we consciously have to engage our compassion. This is clearly a risk for more senior leaders in a company.

Yet, the marriage between social status and greed is not absolute. In fact, some of the most incredible leaders of our time—across industry, government, sport, etc.—displayed remarkable compassion. Patagonia CEO Rose Marcario, German Chancellor Angela Merkel, and Manchester United forward Marcus Rashford all embody this blend of status and compassion. In this new digital age of connection and complexity, compassion becomes even more important as leaders try to harness talent from the global community.

THE COMPASSIONATE LEADER'S TOOLBELT

Since compassion requires action, it does require a willingness to step back and then **B.A.M.!**

B is for Brave. Compassion involves action, which entails risk. When there's no wind—or no one within our reach in need—we don't need the courage; it can sit in reserve. But when the winds kick up, we need to call on this courage to move us to action. For children, this courage can often be easy. They stand up for other kids because they have a strong sense of justice—and are not fully calculating consequences.

A is for Affiliation. Our connection with one another guides our actions in compassion to help figure out the best solution. If we want to be compassionate, we must disregard our judgments and assumptions to listen to the other person and gain a full account of their experience. Adults are terrible at this—when someone needs help, I find that most adults go straight to advice mode. We are very good at telling others what we think they should do. If they don't follow our advice, we love to say, "I told you so."

Children don't act in this way—they are always exploring ways to connect. When a child talks ad nauseam about their favorite show or watches you doing something over your shoulder and asks one billion questions, they are seeking connection. Most important in this is that children haven't established mental models about people. They think everyone is worthy of connection. If you want to compare that to adults, consider how many specialized dating websites exist—from FarmersOnly .com to StarTrekDating.com.

The leader here needs to tap into an old concept: manage by walking around (MBWA)—either virtually or in person—seeking moments where the only point is connection. Here, your curiosity and authenticity superpowers will serve you well.

M is for Mindful. We must be interested and invested in what others are saying. This isn't necessarily solving their problems for them—but being mindful and caring about them in the sense of displaying a genuine concern for others. Acknowledging that everyone struggles, including ourselves, we can demonstrate care by simply recognizing someone else's pain and responding to it.

This requires a leader to lean into knowing their employees on both a professional and personal level. It is about creating a culture where it is safe for people to share their struggles without fear. It is also about the stories we choose to tell—which should include when someone showed us compassion.

It's about seeing the Marcuses around us.

A THREAT TO B.A.M.!

Adults rarely make use of this tool belt—since being compassionate is filled with real, cognitive trade-offs. In fact, the Bystander Effect is a toxic byproduct of this. The Bystander Effect is when a person does nothing to help someone in need because of the presence of others. When the welfare of the suffering person is deemed overwhelmingly difficult to improve, we will adjust our thinking to match our inaction.

We question our understanding of a situation, so much so that we say nothing—amplifying the injustice and further isolating the victim. It's a tragedy. If we had the courage to see the pain and step in, we would probably save a lot of mental, emotional, and, perhaps, physical energy.

Leaders need to be willing to take the risk. Compassion can come in a variety of shapes and sizes. It may involve a leave of absence, a temporary reassignment, or some other action that maintains the employee's self-worth while alleviating their pain.

For leaders, compassion can be a challenge because there are no easy answers. We don't like working at things without definitive solutions—the complexity can be daunting. Being compassionate does not mean *solving* the problems of others, though. It means listening to them, hearing them, and helping find a solution that *eases* their pain. It is an abstract idea with ill-defined parameters; it's quite messy, like the world itself, and yet, it is necessary for us to foster a better world.

In fact, none of the other superpowers in this book matter without compassion. We are a tribal species, and we get all the big things done that enable us to survive and thrive when we work together. No matter how many curious, resilient, authentic individuals are walking around, if we don't figure out how to work collectively, we are dead meat. Every superhero is a superhero because they take action to serve others. They put their own comfort aside and take risks in order to serve the greater good. Nobody becomes a superhero without compassion.

ADDITIONAL INSIGHT FROM THE LAB

Multiple studies have tied perceived suffering to personal distress, a response in which one is more upset by the other's suffering than concerned for the other.[54]

In affective empathy, a person experiences elements of feeling that are similar to another's emotion. "While affective empathy may be considered a catalyst to feeling compassion, affective empathy does not guarantee, nor is it sufficient to engender, compassion. In fact, affective empathy can easily initiate self-focused responses."[55]

Alas, like all scientific studies in the nineteenth century, Darwin's theories have been honed through rigorous study by his successors. In the 1960s, biologist Lynn Margulis came up with a theory of survival through collaboration—noting that two eukaryotic cells once merged with prokaryotic cells, which began the rapid expansion of multicellular life.[56] In our own bodies, there are over 10,000 organisms that enable us to survive every day. In fact, only 43 percent of our body's cells are human cells; the rest are microbial stowaways needed to maintain the ecosystem that keeps us alive.[57] Doesn't sound like "every man for himself."

Paul Bloom, a Yale psychologist, notes that extending empathy to abstract strangers is a particular challenge for the human mind.[58]

Originally described by the Stoics thousands of years ago, the concept of "oikeiōsis" describes how our empathy and affinity for others declines by proximity to our lives. Imagine a series of rings: in the bullseye, there's the self, the innermost ring represents one's family, the next ring represents one's friends, the next represents one's neighbors, then one's tribe or community, then one's country, and so on.

The problem, says Bloom, comes when bad actors hijack these "circles of sympathy" to try and sway our behaviors and beliefs. Our natural empathy for those closer and more similar to us can be harnessed to provoke antipathy towards those who are not.[59]

LATER THAT DAY...

ALL RIGHT, JOSE, SO TOMORROW YOU'LL BRING ME DETAILS ON...

⟨GULP!⟩

WOULD YOU LIKE TO TALK ABOUT IT?

I'M SORRY. MY MOTHER IS VERY ILL AND I'VE BEEN TAKING CARE OF HER. IT'S BEEN STRESSFUL AND TAKES UP A LOT OF MY EVENINGS. I'M FEELING A BIT BURNED OUT.

I'M SORRY TO HEAR ABOUT YOUR MOTHER AND THAT YOU'RE FEELING THIS WAY. DO YOU HAVE ANOTHER FIVE MINUTES? LET'S SEE HOW WE CAN ADJUST YOUR WORKLOAD FOR THE TIME BEING.

· · · · ·

CHAPTER FIVE

PLAYFULNESS

One day last spring, I was watching my grandchildren play Dragons and Dinosaurs in a park. As you may recall, Ben made a last, gallant effort to save his fellow Dragons. Play!

Of all the superpowers, "play" is the most fun to say. "Work," on the other hand, sounds so fixed, rigid, and serious. Playfulness, the noun, is described as being light-hearted or full of fun. While play appears to be a good time, in the never-ending to-do list of adulthood, play might seem like a colossal waste of time. In the end, do we really want to encourage managers and leaders to be playful?

Play, or playfulness, is the final superpower and a fitting capstone to our journey, which began with curiosity, as there is a natural connection between the two.

Play is to work as finger painting is to coloring by numbers. Coloring by numbers, with its rules and lines, is restrictive, with a clear end in mind; it's so outcome-driven. Conversely, finger painting is liberating—a little red (creativity), some blue (imagination), let's grab some yellow (curiosity), and why not some green (laughter), and you have this messy thing we call "play."

It is hard to discuss play without bringing in imagination and creativity. Play is the physical exercise of the imagination. Being able to use symbolic substitutes for real objects is at the core of imagination. Imagination is not only an essential ingredient for play but an expected outcome.

Let's explore the verb "to play," its value, and what's happening to it. We will then turn our attention to playfulness and focus on its quality as a leadership trait.

THE VALUE OF PLAY

One of the more transformational studies of child's play comes from Russian psychiatrist Lev Vygotsky, who stated, "In play, a child is always above his average age, above his daily behavior; in play, it is as though he were a head taller than himself."[60]

There are a number of interpretations of Vygotsky's meaning when it comes to children as they develop. What is not in dispute is that Vygotsky is, as we are here, talking about one type of playfulness: make-believe and unstructured play. Unstructured by adults, but perhaps structured by the children themselves, with negotiated rules, identified roles, and chosen sides.

As we will see, the paradox of play is that while it may look silly and frivolous, it offers, when *unstructured,* a number of benefits for children and adults alike.

It is in this make-believe world that real-world cognitive development occurs. Vygotsky notes, "Play is a transitional stage. At the critical moment when a stick becomes a horse, one of the basic psychological structures determining the child's relationship to reality is radically altered."[61]

Play also overrides instant gratification. In our opening story about Ben, his fellow Dragons were on the swing sets, or, as they called it, in jail. Clearly, they could run off whenever they wanted, so why wait? Observing the rules of the game brings greater joy than the easy relief of freedom. A fascinating aspect of child's play is the unwritten rules by which most participants willingly abide.

Play facilitates the ability to see others' perspectives—or what is called "cognitive decentering." In pretend play, children adroitly assign roles ("I'm a Dragon") and make use of props ("This wrapping paper tube is your sword"). Perspective-taking occurs because the child playing the Dragon is aware of the imaginary sword and proclamations of the Dragon Slayer. In fact, children can easily switch roles because they're able to readily summon the appropriate perspective.

It also appears that play seems to offer the best available means to rein in the feelings of superiority associated with narcissism. Significant data correlates a reduction in playtime and an increase in narcissism in college students.[62] Given the growing emphasis on external versus intrinsic rewards, the scale is tipped for activities that deliver a tangible reward. Unstructured play, almost by definition, provides solely intrinsic rewards.

Paradoxically, play is at the same time both meritocratic and egalitarian. Its meritocracy is simple: if you are good at the game, everyone will know. Measuring each other also works if you are not so good, a judgment that rewards with humility. Play can be an egalitarian activity, and when it requires a larger number of players, it often moves children to work for harmony so that "the game can go on."

The final value of play comes from a list of regrets of the dying. Bronnie Ware is an Australian nurse who spent several years working in palliative care, caring for patients in the last twelve weeks of their lives. She recorded their dying epiphanies and compiled them in a book called *The Top Five Regrets of the Dying*.[63]

Two of the top five make a direct line to play: "I wish I hadn't worked so hard" and "I wish I had let myself be happier."[64] It appears if we all play more, we will have fewer regrets when our time comes to tap out.

Often, when adults do appear to play, it involves achieving a result: staying in shape, losing five pounds, or improving teamwork. As Jeff Harry, a positive-play coach who works with businesses, says, "With adults it's always, 'What am I getting out of this?'"[65] Play appears to have no tangible result; it is its own reward.

THE STATE OF PLAY TODAY

What is the state of play? Why don't adults play more, and why are children playing less? Is it possible children are finding this superpower harder to come by?

Lately, childhood play, from the toy room to the classroom, has gotten hit with numerous arrows, which, ultimately, have found their way to the boardroom.

The first arrow hits everywhere: it's the culture itself. Almost all cultures perform a formal transition from childhood to adulthood. These transitions carry an underlying theme that childhood is over, and we are now adults. A famous biblical passage says, "When I was a child, I spoke and thought and reasoned as a child. But when I grew up, I put away childish things." (1 Corinthians 13:11 New Living Translation). The Puritans, who played an outsized role in American culture, would certainly have considered playing a "childish thing." The result is a cutting off, not only of childhood itself but, sadly, also some of the key attributes we treasure in children.

Fast forward from the Puritans to a culture that prioritizes child safety, and you have schizophrenia in raising children; unfettered access to the internet is okay (because it's in the home) but riding a bike without a helmet (outside) is too risky. The idea that you may not know where your ten-year-old is on a Saturday afternoon is routinely judged as parental neglect.

The culture fills our minds with self-defeating kryptonite with messages like:

- It's too risky.

- I will look foolish.

- There is no time.

- People will think I'm a flake.

- Play needs to be structured and organized.

- Unsupervised play is risky.

Speaking of childish things to put away, how about video games? We all know that adults who play video games need to grow up and leave their parents' basement, and video games will be our ruination, right?

The majority of gamers are now over thirty-three years old.[66] Recent studies have shown that adults who play video games have higher levels of happiness.[67] Sure, they're happier. Sitting around doing nothing, why they're—wait for it—playing! This playing, however, builds a connection to their inner child, which makes them better equipped to deal with stress because they gain exposure to greater creativity and imagination.

In the gaming world, there is no such thing as an impossible challenge, and all failure is temporary. This ethos creates a consistent sense of optimism among gamers, which is not necessarily easy to summon in the real world. Even from behind their consoles, studies show that gamers also can benefit from genuine social support and connections.[68]

The second arrow is launched from the makers of toys and games. An industry that should be an ally has quietly conspired to structure play. Historically, LEGO blocks offered unlimited potential and the opportunity for imagination. A coalition of marketing and merchandising has now given us "franchise sets," with detailed instruction books and unique pieces.

Blogger Chris Swan argues that building instructions marked the start of the decline. "LEGO taught me the art of creative destruction, the need to break something in order to make something better," he writes. "Single-outcome sets encourage preservation rather than destruction, and sadly, that makes them less useful, less educational (and, in my opinion, less fun)."[69]

It's not just LEGO. Educational toys have also blurred the line and perhaps created an environment in which non-educational toys are of lesser value. An educational toy should result in intellectual growth. But while it may bring peace of mind to know that your offspring is "getting smarter," it risks crowding out the benefits of unstructured play. Today, more toys are designed to educate and develop the child than ever before.

Guess which educational toys do best? It turns out that researchers have discovered that *basic is better since these kinds of toys foster the creativity inherent in play*. The highest-scoring toys have been quite simple: hardwood blocks, wooden vehicles, and the classic wooden construction toys most adults of a certain age remember with fondness. These toys are relatively open-ended, so children can use them in multiple ways.[70]

Our final arrow targets adults and is due to the growth of technology. Technology, which enables great efficiency and productivity, has caused serious pain. Many of us can work from anywhere at any time. If you work from home, it may feel like you never really leave the office. Holding a computer in your pocket that is constantly connected to your work email can make it feel impossible to ever truly be off the clock.

If we are never "off the clock," we don't have the time for creativity. When we're tired after work, our brain is less efficient at focusing on a task. Yet, the tired brain is perfect for insight problems. It's one of the reasons great ideas can happen in the shower after a long day. Checking email at 10:00 p.m. rarely sparks genius.

This "always-on" mode doesn't result in better work. Instead, it leads to burnout, lack of sleep, and depression. The proverb "All work and no play makes Jack a dull boy" implies that without time off from work, a person becomes both bored and boring. However, in reality, the opposite of play is not work or even seriousness; it's depression.

Luka Gorse, author of *Feel Like Superhuman*, notes, "Year after year overworked and overstressed people come to me for advice on feeling optimal. And for years I have been giving them advices like: increase your sleep quota, eat better . . . , meditate . . . It's not that these are bad advices. It's that they are just a small part of the big picture . . . But for others who have asked me: 'What is the single most important thing you would advise to reduce stress?' I would answer simply 'Just be more playful.'"[71]

PLAY AND PLAYFULNESS AT WORK

A study of 1.4 million people in 166 countries revealed that the frequency of laughter among all groups plummets around age twenty-three, right about the age most people enter the full-time workforce. As Jennifer Aaker and Naomi Bagdonas explain in their book *Humor, Seriously*, "Before long, we lose levity entirely in a sea of bottom lines, slide decks, and mind-numbing conference calls."[72]

In *A Whole New Mind*, Daniel Pink argues that a seismic shift in work is happening in the advanced world. He states, "Ours has been the age of the 'knowledge worker,' the well-educated manipulator and deployer of expertise."[73]

He posits that we are now entering the Conceptual Age, which will require creators and empathizers. The winners in this new age will be those who embrace concepts such as story, design, meaning, and, yes, play.[74]

Yet, we tend to continue to undervalue experimentation and play and overvalue data generation and data analytics. "Work" is formally defined as "activity involving mental or physical effort done in order to achieve a purpose or result"[75]—how serious that sounds.

We live in what has been called a VUCA world (volatile, uncertain, complex, and ambiguous). The pace and rate of change have forced many to reevaluate the traits needed for success. Specialization is out; generalization is in. Gantt charts are dead; agile planning rules. Learning requires an environment where exploration and experimentation are prized, which is also the type of climate where play and imagination thrive.

Still, play and playfulness at work are nothing new. From team-building exercises to game rooms as an employee benefit, employers attempt to find ways to bring play into the job. The assumption is that the play environment will attract and retain talent while also increasing creativity and innovation—but is that true?

Much of the conceptualization for game rooms comes from Silicon Valley. Betson, a distributor of arcade and amusement equipment, assures us that "a lounge space can be a critical part of an optimally performing office design while enhancing company culture. Because of their team building effectiveness, their value as recruitment tools, and serious scientific literature explaining their health benefits, employee game rooms are a staple of the world's top companies."[76]

This view contrasts sharply with Dan Lyons's opinion in *Disrupted: My Misadventure in the Start-Up Bubble*. Lyons refers to this kind of workplace as "a cross between a kindergarten and a frat house."[77] What's more, all of the video, arcade, and table games in the world cannot outweigh the impact of one disengaged manager.

And how about team building? We would argue the basic premise is misbegotten. Team-building exercises are based on the premise that if team members spent more time doing silly things and solving problems together (doing improv, writing a song, or climbing a wall), they would work more effectively together the rest of the time. Here is a great story illustrating how bad this idea can be:

A new manager who inherited a production unit pulled a culture team together and asked them to come up with something to solve the "engagement problem." The team met and recommended a Saturday beer and softball game, and the manager agreed it would help with motivation.

Real play evokes voluntarism and invites instant openness; often, neither of these is present in the world of corporate team building. Here's what the manager learned on that fateful Saturday: there's only one thing worse than a disgruntled, unmotivated, sober employee: a disgruntled, unmotivated, **drunk** employee . . . with a baseball bat!

It turns out motivation and engagement have less to do with leather gloves to catch softballs and far more to do with leaders who can laugh.

The adult trait of playfulness is associated with a broad range of positive outcomes, such as academic success, coping with stress, innovative work performance, and subjective well-being.[78] Both adults and adolescents are attracted to playful people—just like kids.

We are not recommending playfulness for mate selection here. What we are arguing is that it's a desirable trait in both men and women and can be effectively applied at work. Basically, we all need to be a little more Tony Stark/Iron Man, with his boundless energy, enthusiasm, imagination—and playfulness.

In the evolving relationship between Tony Stark and Peter Parker, a.k.a. Spiderman, Tony sees his role as part-mentor/coach. In *Spiderman: Homecoming*, Peter has just come off his first real superhero assignment, and Tony, to keep him grounded, offers him this playful advice: "Don't do anything I *would* do, and definitely don't do anything I wouldn't do. There's a little gray area in there, and that's where you operate."[79]

Let's move to playfulness in the manager and leader roles.

In *Performance Breakthrough: A Radical Approach to Success at Work*, Cathy Salit shares a helpful anecdote:

> Andy Grove tells the story of how he and Gordon Moore used imaginative play to turn Intel around at a critical moment in the company's history. Intel had become successful by making memory chips for computers, yet in the early 1980s the Japanese were producing high quality and lower cost chips.

There was clearly a need for another product line. However, the whole organization was built to manufacture and sell memory chips. They were stuck in a corporate rut.

One day, Grove and Moore had a conversation in which it was clear that if they did not solve this problem the board of directors would fire them and find someone who could. They then asked, "What do we think these new executives would do differently?" They quickly agreed that they would "fire" themselves, leave the office and come back in as the new smarter executives. They pretend played. Immediately after this little moment of make-believe the answer was crystal clear. They needed to move out of memory chips and into designing and creating microprocessors—for which Intel is now famous.[80]

Pablo Picasso, one of the most important art figures of the twentieth century, is known in part for exploring and inventing a number of styles. There is something uniquely spontaneous about his most famous works. Perhaps he captured this super-power best when he famously said, "It took me four years to paint like Raphael but a lifetime to paint like a child."

Unconvinced on the importance of play and imagination? How about people working for intelligence agencies, people weighed down by life-and-death decision-making? I mean, we don't want them to be playful. Or do we?

It is now generally understood that, in fact, they do need this quality. The 911 Commission that studied the terrorist attack on the United States did not pull any punches when they stated, "The most important failure [of the intelligence agencies] was one of imagination."[81] The people whose job was to keep us safe did not *imagine* terrorists using airplanes as explosive devices.

This is not an isolated example. Guess what the Joint Committee of Congress that investigated the attack on Pearl Harbor found? They also cited a lack of imagination when identifying the failures in leadership: "There is no substitute for imagination and resourcefulness on the part of supervisory and intelligence officials."[82]

Though intelligence officials did initially get defensive when it came to the failure-of-imagination charge, they later started to pursue more "imaginative" measures, such as arranging for analysts to meet with science-fiction writers and directors and screenwriters from Hollywood.

The conclusion the CIA Deputy Director for Intelligence captures nicely is the importance of a work culture that encourages imagination, not only for the CIA but perhaps for any serious endeavor. He says, "To truly nurture creativity, you have to cherish your contrarians, and you have to give them opportunities to run free. Leaders in the analytic community must avoid trying to make everyone meet a preconceived notion of the intelligence community's equivalent of the man in the grey flannel suit."[83]

GOTTA HAVE A TOOLBELT, RIGHT?

What does playfulness look like on a day-to-day basis? Well, it is, at its core, taking oneself a little less seriously and, in doing so, creating a culture where others can do the same. For example, former US Secretary of State Madeleine Albright wore eye-catching pins to be more relatable and spark some humor or joy while performing her diplomatic duties. A consultant colleague of mine, when she falls short of her own high standards, will tell others, "Yep, I shanked it! I am a shankapotamus." Others are then free to smile, laugh, and be human together. (By the way, any word melded with hippo-potamus is just fun.)

Laughter is a big part of being merry; it releases stress hormones and triggers endorphins. The simple act of laughing with others fosters a sense of contagious camaraderie.

This is not about becoming someone people don't take seriously. This is about finding a way to embrace your childlike power and sense of joy. The goal can be to accessorize the **M.A.S.K.** of

Metrics, Analytics, Statistics, and Key Performance Indicators (KPIs) with ornamentation that represents your best **M**erry, **A**ccessible, **S**pontaneous, **K**indergarten self.

What is the right tool when we problem-solve and brainstorm? The Board of Innovation gets it partly right when they say, "Ideation is not just a matter of getting the right people in the room, adding some post-its and beers to the mix, and waiting for three hours until the next disruptive venture is somehow brought into being."[84] But they throw kryptonite when they say, "A good ideation session is hard work! It is a structured process of guiding the right people through a number of carefully designed exercises to come up with innovative ideas."[85] Yippee. Sounds like hell.

A good ideation session should be playful. It should be flavored with BAM!—a dollop of competition, POW!—a dash of silliness, and KRAK!—a cup and a half of laughter. We should make it our goal in these sessions to ZLOPP!!—color way outside the lines.

ADDITIONAL INSIGHT FROM THE LAB

F ortunately, play is much studied, and there is clear value to this "useless behavior." Most influential current research into the relationship between play and learning suggests that play behaviors are motivated by learners' moment-to-moment epistemic curiosity—the desire to obtain information.

A recent study of childhood development begins with the following language: "In thinking about play, we are particularly struck by the profligacy with which children set seemingly arbitrary rewards and incur unnecessary costs . . . and why it might be useful to engage in apparently useless behavior."[86]

The *American Journal of Play* details not only how much children's playtime has declined, but how this privation of play affects emotional development: "Over the past half-century, in the United States and other developed nations, children's free play with other children has declined sharply. Over the same period, anxiety, depression, suicide, feelings of helplessness and narcissism have increased sharply in children, adolescents and young adults."[87]

"Since about 1955 . . . children's free play has been continually declining, at least partly because adults have exerted ever-increasing control over children's activities,"[88] says author Peter Gray, Ph.D., Professor of Psychology (emeritus) at Boston College. Parents who hover over and intrude on their children's play are a big part of the problem, according to Gray. "It is hard to find groups of children outdoors at all, and, if you do find them, they are likely to be wearing uniforms and following the directions of coaches while their parents dutifully watch and cheer."[89]

A study by Chick et al. of adults suggests that both males and females consider playfulness a highly desirable trait in potential partners, as they also consider desirable those who are fun-loving and who have a sense of humor. Participants in a study of adolescents were asked to nominate five strengths in an ideal partner. Both boys (77.5 percent) and girls (76.5 percent) rated the strength of *humor-playfulness* only below honesty. They ranked the strengths of *love, kindness,* and *hope* third to fifth.[90]

The psychologist Rene Proyer has identified four basic types of playful adults: "There are people who like to fool around with friends and acquaintances. We describe this as other-directed playfulness. By contrast, light-heartedly playful people regard their whole life as a type of game," says Proyer. Another grouping includes people who like to play with thoughts and ideas: intellectual playfulness. These people are able to turn monotonous tasks into something interesting. The psychologist describes the final group as being whimsically playful. "These people tend to be interested in strange and unusual things and are amused by small day-to-day observations."[91]

Comic strips by Scott Mooney with inks by Nick Crain

AFTERWORD

So, there they are—The Five Lost Superpowers.

Given the subject matter, when the four authors got together, it was difficult not to think about the Fantastic Four as a potential group name. It turns out this definition was prescient because Wikipedia describes the Fantastic Four as follows: "the Fantastic Four have been portrayed as a somewhat dysfunctional, yet loving, family."[92] This is us to a tee.

There was healthy debate and exploration regarding the identity of the five superpowers. You may be rightly asking yourself, what about risk-taking? (more a teenager thing); creativity? (it's part of playfulness); grit and tenacity? (they are embedded in resilience). Where is mindfulness?! (it is critical to compassion.) And finally, what about honesty? (Children can be brutally honest; honesty is captured in authenticity.)

We encourage you to reintroduce yourself to these "lost" super-powers. You don't need to be around children to activate what already exists (although it does help). Speeding trains and tall buildings await—start soaring.

ACKNOWLEDGMENTS

Every wildly popular *Avengers* movie explores the boundless power of teamwork. Even superheroes are made better and stronger by a good team. We would like to acknowledge those on our team who made us better throughout this process. Thank you to our editor, Dr. Steven Hart, for his keen eye and generous spirit. Thank you to Alex Nates-Perez for the devoted care you gave to us and to this project. A final thank you to Kelley Nicholson, Casey Shiley, and Kate Reid, who gave us their wisdom and support as they reacted to draft chapters.

ABOUT THE AUTHORS

JOHN REID

John Reid is the Founder, President, and lead designer of JMReid Group, a global behavior change organization specializing in leadership, development, sales effectiveness, and skill enhancement. After John survived three bouts of cancer, he decided to pursue his passion for learning and development. John pursued this passion with the belief that people want to get better and can get better. JMRG is founded on the principle that the learner and their success is our reason to be.

LYNAE STEINHAGEN

Lynae Steinhagen is a consultant, facilitator, trainer, and coach. Reading Victor Frankl taught her this: "Between stimulus and response, there is a space. In that space is our power to choose our response. In our response lies our growth and our freedom." She's convinced that the many joys of her life come from responding with a choice to keep going and a fervent belief that things will get better. Lynae lives in Minnesota with her husband, Jim, and their dog, Rocket.

CORENA CHASE

Corena Chase is an executive coach, trainer, and facilitator. She has spent her life exploring what it means to be authentic: as a child who distressed adults by sniffing out inauthenticity in authority figures; as an actor who worked to present authentic portrayals of who we are; as a human navigating the least authentic city in America, Hollywood; and as a coach working with others to explore and embrace the full (super)power of their authentic selves.

ANDREW REID

Andrew believes in the inherent goodness in people. Having taught for five years in urban and suburban schools in the Philadelphia region, he has witnessed the predisposition young children have for creating kind, equitable, and compassionate spaces. He has also experienced the forces that work against these ideals firsthand. Throughout his experience as a teacher, he became skilled at working with kids across all spectrums of diversity to bring excitement to the classroom, engage them in learning, and help them grow a safe-classroom community. He brings these abilities to JMReid Group to create and deliver world-class programs.

Andrew and his wife, Lynn, live in Bucks County, Pennsylvania, with their three sons. He received his M.Ed. from Chestnut Hill College and two bachelor of arts degrees from the University of Maryland and Rutgers University.

ENDNOTES

1 Sara Lynn Hua, "Difference between a Chinese Dragon and a Western Dragon," *TutorMing China Expats & Culture Blog*, June 28, 2016, http://blog.tutorming .com/expats/chinese-dragon-western-difference-lucky.

2 Sarah Whitten, "The 13 Highest-Grossing Film Franchises at the Box Office," CNBC, January 31, 2021, https://www.cnbc.com/2021/01/31/the-13-highest-grossing-film-franchises-at-the-box-office.html.

3 *The Wizard of Oz*, directed by Richard Thorpe, Victor Fleming, and King Vidor (Culver City, CA: Metro-Goldwyn-Mayer, 1939).

4 Mel Robbins, "How to Stop Screwing Yourself Over," presented at TEDxSF, San Francisco, CA, 2011, https://www.ted.com/talks/mel_robbins_how_to_stop _screwing_yourself_over.

5 Susan Engel, "Children's Need to Know: Curiosity in Schools," *Harvard Educational Review* 81, no. 4 (December 2011): 625–45.

6 Michelle M. Chouinard, "Children's Questions: A Mechanism for Cognitive Development," Monographs *of the Society for Research in Child Development* 72, no. 1 (2007): i–129.

7 Thomas Szasz, Words to the Wise: A Medical-Philosophical Dictionary (New York: Routledge, 2004), 40.

8 Susan Engel, *The Hungry Mind: The Origins of Curiosity in Childhood* (Cambridge: Harvard University Press, 2015), 88.

9 Malcolm Gladwell, *Outliers: The Story of Success* (New York: Little, Brown and Company, 2008).

10 David Epstein, Range: Why Generalists Triumph in a Specialized World (New York: Riverhead Books, 2019).

11 Epstein, *Range*.

12 Todd B. Kashdan, "What Are the Five Dimensions of Curiosity?" *Psychology Today*, January 2, 2018, https://www.psychologytoday.com/us/blog/curious/201801/what-are-the-five-dimensions-curiosity.

13 Bertrand Russell, "How to Grow Old," in *Portraits from Memory and Other Essays* (New York: Simon & Schuster, 1956), 50–53.

14 Megan Schmidt, "How Reading Fiction Increases Empathy And Encourages Understanding," *Discover Magazine*, August 28, 2020, https://www.discovermagazine.com/mind/how-reading-fiction-increases-empathy-and-encourages-understanding.

15 Heidrick and Struggles, The CEO Report: Embracing the Paradoxes of Leadership and the Power of Doubt (New York: Heidrick and Struggles, 2014).

16 Charlotte Ruhl, "Theory of Mind," *Simply Psychology*, August 7, 2020, https://www.simplypsychology.org/theory-of-mind.html.

17 Alison Gopnik and Ezra Klein, "Why Adults Lose the 'Beginner's Mind,'" April 16, 2021, in *The Ezra Klein Show*, produced by *The New York Times*, podcast, 1:03:33, https://www.nytimes.com/2021/04/16/opinion/ezra-klein-podcast-alison-gopnik.html.

18 Joan Littlefield Cook and Greg Cook, "Chapter 5: Cognitive Development: Piagetian and Sociocultural Views," in *Child Development* (Boston: Allyn & Bacon, 2005), 5-3–5-24.

19 Jean Piaget, *The Psychology of Intelligence* (New York: Littlefield, Adams, 1969).

20 Jaak Panksepp, Affective Neuroscience: The Foundations of Human and Animal Emotions (New York: Oxford University Press, 1998).

21 Robert M. Sapolsky, *Behave: The Biology of Humans at Our Best and Worst* (New York: Penguin Books, 2017).

22 Carol S. Dweck, *Mindset: The New Psychology of Success* (New York: Random House, 2006).

23 Guy Raz and Carol Dweck, "Should We Stop Telling Kids They're Smart?" TED Radio Hour, June 24, 2016, https://www.npr.org/transcripts/483126798.

24 Names have been changed to protect their privacy.

25 Jon Winokur, *Writers on Writing* (Philadelphia: Running Press, 1986).

26 Ann S. Masten, Karin M. Best, and Norman Garmezy, "Resilience and Development: Contributions from the Study of Children Who Overcome Adversity," *Development and Psychopathology* 2, no. 4 (1990): 425–44.

27 Alison Pearce Stevens, "Learning Rewires the Brain," *Science News for Students*, September 2, 2014, https://www.sciencenewsforstudents.org/article/learning-rewires-brain.

28 Princeton University, "Infants Use Expectations to Shape Their Brains," *Eureka Alert*, American Association for the Advancement of Science, July 20, 2015, https://www.eurekalert.org/pub_releases/2015-07/pu-iue072015.php.

29 Sasha Emmons, "How to Build Healthy Self-Esteem in Children," *Scholastic Parents*, accessed April 26, 2021, https://www.scholastic.com/parents/family-life/social-emotional-learning/praise-and-discipline/how-to-build-healthy-self-esteem-children.html.

30 Emmy Werner, "High-Risk Children in Young Adulthood: A Longitudinal Study from Birth to 32 Years," *American Journal of Orthopsychiatry* 59, no. 1 (1989): 72–81.

31 Emmy E. Werner and Ruth S. Smith, *Overcoming the Odds: High-Risk Children from Birth to Adulthood* (New York: Cornell University Press, 1992).

32 "Martin Seligman," *Pursuit of Happiness*, accessed April 26, 2021, https://www.pursuit-of-happiness.org/history-of-happiness/martin-seligman-psychology/.

33 Martin E. P. Seligman, Flourish: A Visionary New Understanding of Happiness and Well-being (New York: Free Press, 2011).

34 Kim Armstrong, "Remarkable Resiliency: George Bonanno on PTSD, Grief, and Depression," *Convention Coverage*, Association for Psychological Science, January 29, 2020, https://www.psychologicalscience.org/observer/bonanno.

35 Harvard Medical School, "Exercising to Relax," *Harvard Men's Health Watch*, February 2011 (updated July 7, 2020), https://www.health.harvard.edu/staying-healthy/exercising-to-relax.

36 Eun Joo Kim, Blake Pellman, and Jeansok J. Kim, "Stress Effects on the Hippocampus: A Critical Review," *Learning and Memory* 22, no. 9 (September 2015): 411–16.

37 Saul McLeod, "Stress, Illness and the Immune System," *Simply Psychology*, updated 2010, https://www.simplypsychology.org/stress-immune.html.

38 Heather S. Lonczak, Ph.D, "30+ Tips for Building Resilience in Children," *Positive Psychology*, January 9, 2020, https://positivepsychology.com/resilience -in-children/.

39 Urie Bronfenbrenner, *The Ecology of Human Development: Experiments by Nature and Design* (Cambridge: Harvard University Press, 1979).

40 William S. Ryan and Richard M. Ryan, "Toward a Social Psychology of Authenticity: Exploring Within-Person Variation in Autonomy, Congruence, and Genuineness Using Self-Determination Theory," *Review of General Psychology* 23, no. 1 (April 26, 2019): 99–112.

41 Walt Whitman, "Song of Myself, 51," in *Leaves of Grass*, stanza 3, line 8.

42 Ryan and Ryan, "Toward a Social Psychology of Authenticity."

43 Serena Chen, "Authenticity in Context: Being True to Working Selves," *Review of General Psychology* 23, no. 1 (April 26, 2019): 61.

44 Ryan and Ryan, "Toward a Social Psychology of Authenticity."

45 *Oxford Learner's Dictionaries*, s.v. "authenticity (*noun*)," accessed April 26, 2021, https://www.oxfordlearnersdictionaries.com/us/definition/american _english/authenticity.

46 Mencius, *Mengzi*, trans. Bryan W. Van Norden (Indianapolis: Hackett Publishing Company, 2008), 46.

47 Max McClure, "Infants Process Faces Long before They Recognize Other Objects, Stanford Vision Researchers Find," *Stanford News*, December 11, 2012, https://news.stanford.edu/news/2012/december/infants-process-faces -121112.html.

48 Umberto Castiello, Cristina Becchio, Stefania Zoia, Cristian Nelini, Luisa Sartori, Laura Blason, Giuseppina D'Ottavio, Maria Bulgheroni, and Vittorio Gallese, "Wired to Be Social: The Ontogeny of Human Interaction," *PLOS ONE* 5, no. 10 (October 7, 2010).

49 Gareth Cook, "The Moral Life of Babies," *Scientific American*, November 12, 2013, https://www.scientificamerican.com/article/the-moral-life-of-babies/.

50 Margarita Svetlova, Sara R. Nichols, and Celia A. Brownell, "Toddlers' Prosocial Behavior: From Instrumental to Empathic to Altruistic Helping," *Child Development* 81, no. 6 (November 15, 2010): 1814–27.

51 Larry Dossey, "The Helper's High" *Explore* 14, no. 6 (November 2018): 393–99.

52 Mike Krings, "Study Shows Decline in Cognitive Empathy among Middle School Students," The University of Kansas, October 3, 2016, https://news.ku.edu/mk%20empathy.

53 Charles Darwin, The Descent of Man and Selection in Relation to Sex (London: John Murray, 1871), 82.

54 C. Daniel Batson, *Altruism in Humans* (New York: Oxford University Press, 2011), 19.

55 Jennifer L. Goetz and Emiliana Simon-Thomas, "The Landscape of Compassion: Definitions and Scientific Approaches," in *The Oxford Handbook of Compassion Science*, ed. Emma M. Seppala, Emiliana Simon-Thomas, Stephanie L. Brown, Monica C. Worline, C. Daryl Cameron, and James R. Doty (New York: Oxford University Press, 2017), 6.

56 Lynn Margulis, "On the Origin of Mitosing Cells," *Journal of Theoretical Biology* 14, no. 3 (March 1967): 255–74.

57 James Gallagher, "More than Half Your Body Is Not Human," *BBC News*, April 10, 2018, https://www.bbc.com/news/health-43674270.

58 Richard Fisher, "The Surprising Downsides of Empathy," *BBC Future*, October 1, 2020, https://www.bbc.com/future/article/20200930-can-empathy-be-bad-for-you.

59 Fisher, "The Surprising Downsides of Empathy."

60 Lev Vygotsky, "Play and Its Role in the Mental Development of the Child," *Soviet Psychology* 5, no. 3 (1967): 6–18.

61 Vygotsky, "Play and Its Role in the Mental Development of the Child."

62 Peter Gray, "The Decline of Play and the Rise of Psychopathology in Children and Adolescents," *American Journal of Play* 3, no. 4 (2011): 443–63.

63 Bronnie Ware, *The Top Five Regrets of the Dying* (Alexandria NSW: Hay House, 2011).

64 Ware, The Top Five Regrets of the Dying.

65 Kristin Wong, "How to Add More Play to Your Grown-Up Life, Even Now," *New York Times*, August 14, 2020, https://www.nytimes.com/2020/08/14/smarter-living/adults-play-work-life-balance.html.

66 Entertainment Software Association (ESA), 2019 Essential Facts about the Computer and Video Game Industry (May 2019), 5.

67 Jason C. Allaire, Anne Collins McLaughlin, Amanda Trujillo, Laura A. Whitlock, LandonLaPorte, and Maribeth Gandy, "Successful Aging through Digital Games: Socioemotional Differences between Older Adult Gamers and Non-Gamers," *Computers in Human Behavior* 29, no. 4 (July 2013): 1302–06.

68 Christian M. Jones, Laura Scholes, Daniel Johnson, Mary Katsikitis, and Michelle C. Carras, "Gaming Well: Links between Videogames and Flourishing Mental Health," *Frontiers in Psychology* 5 (March 2014): 260.

69 Chris Swan, "The Perils of Modern Lego," *Chris Swan's* Weblog, January 1, 2013, https://blog.thestateofme.com/2013/01/01/the-perils-of-modern-lego/.

70 "What the Research Says: Impact of Specific Toys on Play," National Association for the Education of Young Children, accessed April 26, 2021, https://www.naeyc.org/resources/topics/play/specific-toys-play.

71 Luka Gorse, "Seriousness vs. Playfulness," LukaGorse.com, January 7, 2020, http://lukagorse.com/seriousness-vs-playfulness/.

72 Jennifer Aaker and Naomi Bagdonas, Humor, Seriously: Why Humor Is a Secret Weapon in Business and Life and How Anyone Can Harness It. Even You. (New York: Random House, 2021), 22–23.

73 Daniel H. Pink, A Whole New Mind: Why Right-Brainers Will Rule the Future (New York: Riverhead Books, 2005), 2.

74 Pink, A Whole New Mind.

75 *Oxford English Dictionary*, s.v. "work (noun)," accessed April 26, 2021, https://www.lexico.com/en/definition/work.

76 James Liess, "Employee Game Rooms Keep Your Business Ahead of the Competition," *Betson blog*, December 16, 2019, https://www.betson.com/employee-game-rooms/.

77 Dan Lyons, Disrupted: My Misadventure in the Start-Up Bubble (New York: Hachette Books, 2016).

78 René T. Proyer and Lisa Wagner, "Playfulness in Adults Revisited: The Signal Theory in German Speakers," *American Journal of Play* 7, no. 2 (2015): 201–27.

79 *Spiderman: Homecoming*, directed by Jon Watts (Culver City, CA: Sony Pictures Releasing, 2017).

80 Cathy Salit, Performance Breakthrough: A Radical Approach to Success at Work (New York: Hachette Books, 2016).

81 The 911 Commission, The 9/11 Commission Report: Final Report of the National Commission on Terrorist Attacks Upon the United States: Executive Summary (2004), 9.

82 Joint Committee on the Investigation of the Pearl Harbor Attack, *Investigation of the Pearl Harbor Attack* (Washington, D.C.: United States Government Printing Office, 1946), 259.

83 Mike Nartker, "Intelligence Officials Deny Lack of Imagination," *Government Executive*, August 5, 2004, https://www.govexec.com/defense/2004/08/intell igence-officials-deny-lack-of-imagination/17307/.

84 Board of Innovation, "Our Favorite Ideation Tools," Board of Innovation Staff Picks, https://www.boardofinnovation.com/staff_picks/our-favorite-ideation -tools/.

85 Board of Innovation, "Our Favorite Ideation Tools."

86 Junyi Chu and Laura E. Schulz, "Play, Curiosity, and Cognition," *Annual Review of Developmental Psychology* 2 (December 2020): 317–43.

87 Peter Gray, "The Decline of Play and the Rise of Psychopathology in Children and Adolescents," *American Journal of Play* 3, no. 4 (2011): 443.

88 Gray, "The Decline of Play and the Rise of Psychopathology in Children and Adolescents," 444.

89 Gray, "The Decline of Play and the Rise of Psychopathology in Children and Adolescents," 445.

90 René T. Proyer and Lisa Wagner, "Playfulness in Adults Revisited: The Signal Theory in German Speakers," *American Journal of Play* 7, no. 2 (2015): 203–04.

91 René T. Proyer, "A New Structural Model for the Study of Adult Playfulness: Assessment and Exploration of an Understudied Individual Differences Variable," *Personality and Individual Differences* 108 (April 2017): 113–22.

92 Wikipedia, s.v. "Fantastic Four," last modified April 11, 2021, 06:25, https://en .wikipedia.org/wiki/Fantastic_Four.

CPSIA information can be obtained
at www.ICGtesting.com
Printed in the USA
LVHW022039020921
696840LV00003B/41/J

9 781544 522944